D0486443

"I'm on the front lines daily with the codependency and emotional trauma that parents often experience when their child needs or is in treatment and see first-hand the dramatic effect these conditions have on relationships. Far too many parents are torn apart by not having the tools Dr. Reedy provides. This is a must-read for any parent and an awakening for behavioral health professionals."

—*Miles Adcox, CEO, Onsite*

"Brad's compassionate approach invites healing for children and for parents. His ability to help parents and children find their own voice comes as he takes you on the journey of exploring your relationship with yourself and your child. . . . Trusting in his pioneering process is a transformative and healing experience like no other in the field of mental health."

—*Dirk Eldredge, CIP, BRI I, CADAC*
Alchemy Intervention

"Dr. Brad Reedy's dedication to the lives of adolescents and their families is commendable. I often refer families to Second Nature, and have yet to encounter an adolescent or family who has not found the experience to be a life-changing first step on what is often a long and painful journey. I hear nothing but praise from parents for Dr. Reedy's webinars, and this book is a perfect adjunct to those presentations."

—*Teri Solochek, PhD,*
CEP Educational Consultant

"What I love about Brad's work is that he doesn't preach or give advice. Rather, he guides the parent and child through a process of self-discovery. Learning that we have all the wisdom we need, buried beneath our fears, shame, and myriad of voices in our head is an empowering experience."

—*Elisa Hallerman, Founder & CEO,*
Recovery Management Agency

"Dr. Reedy shows us how to parent with an Open Heart. He is able to help parents see through the confusion, frustration, and anxieties to discover the most profound love—the love between a mother and her children."

—Jane Seymour, Emmy & Golden
Globe–winning actress, author,
artist, entrepreneur, and mother

"*The Journey of the Heroic Parent* shows how the generation gap that exists between parents and children can be bridged as a parent embraces his own journey of self discovery."

—Nikki Sixx, bass player, Mötley
Crüe & Sixx Sense radio host

THE JOURNEY OF THE HEROIC PARENT

YOUR CHILD'S STRUGGLE & THE ROAD HOME

Brad M. Reedy, PhD

COFOUNDER AND CLINICAL DIRECTOR,
EVOKE WILDERNESS THERAPY PROGRAMS

Regan Arts.

Regan Arts.

65 Bleecker Street
New York, NY 10012

Originally published in hardcover by Regan Arts in 2015.
First Regan Arts paperback edition, January 2016.

Library of Congress Control Number: 2014955528
ISBN 978-1-68245-002-4

Interior design by Daniel Lagin
Jacket design by Richard Ljoenes

The information in this book is not intended to replace the services of a qualified mental health professional. The author and publisher are not engaged in rendering medical, health, or any other kind of personal professional services in the book.

While the case studies described in this book are based on interviews with real persons, the names, and some professions, locations, and other biographical details about the participants have been changed.

Printed in the United States of America

10   9   8   7   6   5   4   3   2

For Michelle, Jacob, Emma, Isabella, and Olivia:
my wife, my children, my angels

A hero is someone who has given his or her life to something bigger than oneself.

—Joseph Campbell, *The Power of Myth*

CONTENTS

CONTENTS

CONTENTS

CONTENTS

ACKNOWLEDGMENTS

So many people have been a part of the fabric of my life and thus the fabric of this book. There are also those who have walked a path ahead of me who have returned to share their wisdom. There simply isn't space in this book to adequately acknowledge all of the supporters, mentors, and friends who have loved me in a way that has led me to consider that the universe is powered by love.

To my mother: thanks for summoning the strength to take me to therapy and letting me talk about my feelings.

To my Uncle Bob: thank you for being there and seeing me.

Leslie Feinauer, my early mentor, thank you for introducing me to love and acceptance.

Devan Glissmeyer, Vaughn Heath, and Cheryl Kehl: thank you for trusting me and giving me the gift of building such a magical program for children and families.

To the thousands of clients and their families, thank you for inspiring and teaching me about the courage it takes to grow.

To all the professionals whom I call friends, and who have walked beside me on a parallel path: thanks for the work that you do and for the lives you save—one of which is mine.

ACKNOWLEDGMENTS

To Rick Heizer, my muse, you're the one I call to find my center.

To my best friend, Steve, thanks for hanging in there and standing beside me.

Dawn Hansen and Josh Nelson: thanks for your valuable contributions to the final edits of this book.

To my therapist, Jami Gill: I am grateful for your love and wisdom. Thanks for allowing my rotten, horrible self to be okay. Thanks for not being the expert about my life. Thanks for crying when you saw that I had been hurt and I didn't know it. Thanks for finding my river so I could find it myself.

Special thanks also to Pablo Fenjves, Judith Regan, Erin Kelleher, Dirk Eldredge, Jennifer Graham, Lisa VanDyck Euphrat, Kevin Kindlin, Leah Halverson, Patrick Logan, Matt Hoag, Michael Griffin, J Huffine, Brian Shepherd, Malia Shepherd, and Desert Noises.

To my children, my angels, Jake, Emma, Isabella, and Olivia: you are my guardian angels. You have given me a reason not to give up when I wanted to give up.

And lastly to my wife, Michelle: you are my hero. You have loved me when I thought I was unlovable. You have shown a rare courage that has made me want to find myself.

THE HERO IN THE WILDERNESS

WHEN I TEACH PARENTS, OFTEN SOMEONE WILL SAY, "I wish I had this information when my children were young." Unfortunately, when something is not immediately relevant, we usually pay little attention to it. The experience of parenting a struggling child is the most powerful way we learn. It offers us something we cannot get any other way.

The principles contained in this book, drawn from my experiences and observations as a wilderness therapist, apply to parents raising struggling children as well as those whose children are not struggling. Additionally, many of the parents I have taught have also told me that the principles they learned apply to nearly all of their relationships.

In order to understand some of the stories and lessons in this book, it is important to consider my experience as a therapist and parent educator. While this book reaches beyond wilderness therapy and to struggles that all parents encounter, my background will provide both context and jargon.

The summer after my last year of graduate school I worked at a wilderness therapy program in southern Utah. I had previously worked in more traditional settings, including a hospital, community health center, and a private practice, and had no idea what wilderness therapy even was. Furthermore, I couldn't fathom what wilderness had to do with therapy. On my first trip out to meet the group in the wilderness (often called "the field"), I was transported along with the "field staff." I asked the staff to describe wilderness therapy to me. The senior staff member, Charlie, explained, "Most people don't live on the ground. It's like they're living miles above the earth. They are disconnected from the earth and thus disconnected from life, themselves, and each other. We live out here *on* the ground, and that is where you will meet your students."

While it was a rather nebulous description of the model, it made some sense to me. During my undergraduate studies I had taken a class called Temporal Work and Relationships in the Home, which was taught by Dr. Kathleen Bahr. She taught us that many modern advances in our culture are taking us in a dangerous direction. While technology is convenient, there is a hidden cost: we lose the opportunity to teach important life lessons. Our modern conveniences, while time saving, do not advance our humanity. Indeed, it is often through struggle that we learn—through our rituals, our work, and our suffering. Life lessons are intrinsic in living. As the quote by Arnold H. Glasgow goes, "Telling a teenager the facts of life is like giving a fish a bath."

While we contrive and stretch to create teaching moments, primitive cultures rely on oral tradition and modeling to pass on values. Lessons are woven into their religious and daily traditions. One of the challenges when creature comforts are offered too readily to our children is to create similar opportunities for our children to learn. Oftentimes, the lessons seem to them to be contrived—that is, the message seems to be about the parent and not about life. An example may be as simple as this: the old adage, the law of the harvest, "what you reap is what you sow," is easy to understand for the child who grows up on a farm. But a child raised by an attorney may have trouble understanding how that saying applies to the value of trigonometry in twelfth grade.

Dr. Bahr used ice cream as an example. Years ago, ice cream was often made by the whole family. The ingredients were mixed and frozen, and each person would have their turn at the hand crank, keeping an eye on the ice and the salt. The activity might take hours. The entire family was engaged in the same goal, and at the end they each enjoyed the ice cream. Today we buy a half-gallon of ice cream at the grocery store, saving time. But time for what? Usually it is to watch TV or go our separate ways.

Consider the following observation from Harvard anthropology professor Dorothy Lee in 1959:

> When my first child was two or three, I used to shell peas with her. Nowadays, I buy my peas already shelled and packaged. This saves time; and the peas are fresher . . . . But was this all that happened when I shelled peas with my daughter? Did I merely get a dish of peas? It was a total process; and if I am going to see to it that the totality of the important aspects are retained, I shall have to find out what they were and then find the medium through which they can continue to be expressed.

If modern life created some obstacles for parents in the 1950s, imagine the impact our technological advancements have had on today's family.

Students arrive at a wilderness program presenting a variety of issues, such as substance abuse problems, mood disorders, or other mental health issues. Wilderness therapy programs are short-term, primary-care settings that offer families an interruption in the midst of a crisis. Assessment, whether formal or through natural observation, prepares individuals and families for follow-up care settings, which may include outpatient therapy at home, residential programs, or transitional living. Progress in wilderness therapy is dynamic, and research has demonstrated very high levels of retention and generalization.

Our version of wilderness therapy is a nomadic, primitive, small-group-living model. That is a technical way of saying we hike around in the wilderness in groups of eight to ten students, three to four staff members, and a therapist. We set up camp each day in a new area. Licensed therapists meet with the students each week in individual and group therapy sessions and establish treatment plans with the field instructors.

Ours is not an adventure therapy program replete with rappelling, mountain biking, or white-water rafting. While play is an essential part of a balanced life, the use of recreation as the principal modality often serves to soothe parents' guilt when sending their child to a therapeutic program. Adventure therapy can be effective, but if the issue of parental guilt is not addressed, the family will stay stuck in old patterns. In *Nurture Shock*, Bronson and Merryman address the pitfall of an increasing trend of parents replacing hard work with recreation. This trend, they suggest, ensures everybody is happy—but only in the short term. Parents feel less stress, guilt, or personal discomfort, and with their kids entertained and distracted, parents survive to fight another day. Any parent can relate to those motives.

In the primitive living milieu, or "camping therapy," as some call it, the inherent challenges of nature and group living foster community, problem solving, healthy communication, and resiliency. It is neither punitive nor deprivational; instead, it is natural. Nature's elements are the antagonist, and in facing nature's challenges the wilderness student thrives. Some say wilderness therapy living is a metaphor for life, but I find that concept backward. How can living in the natural world be the metaphor and living in the modern world with virtual realities be the "real" world?

Nothing can be taken for granted in the wilderness. Everything comes with work and sacrifice, and often requires compromise, problem solving, and healthy communication between people. Lessons are inherent in the tasks involved. Not listening to field staff might lead to a faulty shelter technique, which would lead to a wet night—no lecture is needed on such an occasion. Students hike, camp, cook, set up shelter, sleep, eat, clean, and carry everything they need on their backs. Fresh food and water are delivered as needed, but the daily task of living lacks the ordinary modern conveniences and creature comforts. Over the years, field instructors have asked me during the difficult winter months, or the rainy seasons of early spring, "How can we do therapy when we are spending so much of the day helping to keep the children safe and warm?"

My response is, "That *is* the therapy." What better way to teach children the importance of patience, responsibility, listening, trust, and frustration tolerance than by nurturing them, caring for them, and teaching them to care for themselves? It relates to everything their parents want them to learn, only you use camping to teach it. The genius of the model is that the lesson comes in through the back door, in a way students don't identify as parental, so the urge to rebel is less likely to be triggered.

The participant in wilderness therapy becomes the hero in his or her own journey: surviving long hikes, making it though a storm, braving cold temperatures, setting up a clean and safe shelter, cooking a meal over a fire *they* built. All these experiences create a sense of accomplishment and efficacy, and in turn these successes increase confidence. Students work together to create camp life. Group sessions throughout the day and weekly sessions with the therapist reference daily living as well as the historical difficulties the child has experienced. The fabric of the therapy is both "here and now" and "then and there." The child can connect the challenges in her day—the challenges she has with staff and peers—to the challenges she experienced at home. Then the lesson becomes about the student herself.

The first thing I learned about children in this environment is that they are much more resilient than they or their parents believed. Wilderness therapy is difficult and, while challenging, it is a safe place to practice living in relation to both others and oneself. Students learn how to feel and how to express their feelings without the usual distractions. Those distractions, or hiding places, are less accessible in the woods. Dealing with the elements positions the child against nature and removes the need to struggle for identity by rejecting parental values.

One of the most common changes for the student in wilderness therapy living is the shift from an external to internal locus of control. This transformation refers to a change from "Happiness and success are determined by the things that happen to me" to "I am the one who determines my happiness and success." Happiness doesn't come when we take our kids to Disneyland (any parent who has journeyed to the Magic Kingdom can attest to that); rather, it comes when we connect to ourselves, work through challenges, and find nurturing in our relationships. Often parents think gratitude comes from abundance; rather, it often comes by working, struggling, and mindfully observing everything. What better place to find and spend time with ourselves than in nature?

Wilderness therapy has evolved over the years. Early versions did not address or support the family. This lack of parental support was one of the principal changes to the model that our program made when it was established in 1998. Our version offers families a plethora of support services. Families can visit the field at the middle and at the end of the course. We also provide cell and satellite phone therapy sessions as student and parents begin to utilize new skills and insights they develop in the weekly letter writing process. Our goal is to treat the identified patient as well as all those affected by their struggles. Weekly phone calls between the wilderness therapist and the parents provide new insights and tools for healthier family living. Weekly letters to and from parents provide a special opportunity to observe family dynamics.

Our deliberate form of family therapy has also offered me a vantage point from which to study the relationships between parents and their children. Through the intimacy of treating their children, I have learned the plight of their parents in raising them. While their stories are often heart-wrenching, their appeals for help are often met with judgment, dogma, and so-called experts selling the "next great thing" in parenting education (which invariably contradicts the last expert). What is missing is a curriculum that helps parents find their truth, buried in their histories and hidden behind the armor they wear to deal with life.

In writing this book, I want to take the lessons learned from my work in the field of wilderness therapy and share them with parents who are struggling to raise children. Rather than promising, "I know what you need to do to fix your child," I offer ideas of how to think about the questions and answers in parenting. This applies to parents of young and adolescent children who are struggling, or anyone interested in the takeaway from families experiencing pain, difficulty, joy, and success.

The work *is* the reward. Becoming a better parent means becoming a better person.

By following this process, we learn to turn our children's lives and successes over to them.

THE
JOURNEY
OF THE
HEROIC
PARENT

CHAPTER ONE

FINDING ONE'S SELF THROUGH PARENTING

We struggle most with our children when they show us something that we were not allowed to feel or do as a child.

IN 2010 I HAD COME TO A CROSSROADS IN MY LIFE. A THIN filament held my marriage together. My wife and I had separated in late May, and I was considering whether to file for divorce or traverse the difficult and painful path of reconciliation. I increased my personal therapy sessions to twice a week in order to navigate this crisis. I also had questions about my career and faced various challenges with my four children (who at that time ranged in age from two to sixteen years old), which further muddled my thinking.

Earlier that year, my wife attended a workshop in Tennessee designed to "re-center" herself. Upon returning, she urged me to sign up for the six-day seminar. I resisted, suspecting this was an attempt to influence me to reconcile. So, I politely declined her suggestion and wandered through that summer and fall in a haze of fear, confusion, and anxiety.

By late fall 2010, it was clear that I wasn't making headway in the struggle that so wholly enveloped me. Clouds of intense anxiety followed brief moments of clarity as I focused on what others wanted from me. Their voices rang so loudly in my thoughts that I could scarcely hear my own, and I continued to wander through the fog of indecision.

Early that winter, an interventionist and another colleague accompanied me on a trip to visit a therapeutic school. While waiting to board the ferry to reach the site, my colleague shared with us that she was considering attending the Tennessee workshop that my wife had attended. Surprised by the coincidence, I found myself confiding in her about the current dilemma I was facing. I admitted that I had considered attending the same workshop. Later I laughed at my decision to share the possibility of my attending a self-improvement workshop in front of an interventionist. As I parried his suggestions with all the excuses I had about why I didn't want to jump into that sort of thing, he did what interventionists do and rejected my doubts with ease. Before I knew it, he had secured a place for me at the workshop, which was less than two weeks away.

I arrived at Nashville Airport in early December and boarded a shuttle to the remote campus. As a co-founder of an experiential program, I felt vulnerable being on the other side of the equation. Because people often hide who they are behind what they do, we were asked to avoid sharing our careers while at the seminar. Still, due to my profession I believed I was in a different position than the rest of the group. I believed that I was the exception to the rule, and I felt naked without the cloak of my career. I then took a deep breath, put aside my reservations, and tried to leave behind the clutter that was blocking me from seeing my inner self.

The shuttle ride was awkward. I was nervous and wondered what kinds of things had brought the others to this place. After settling into our cabins, we reconvened for an orientation. During that introduction, participants began asking questions. Almost everyone had come with one specific personal question, and in a reserved desperation we clamored for answers. I had assumed that my situation was unique, but quickly found several others working through similar processes. The directors assured us that our questions would eventually be addressed—but not yet.

Still, those questions persisted during the first few days. We asked things such as, "Should I stay married?" "Should I change careers?" "How do I deal with my struggling child?" "How do I deal with my alcoholic mother dying of cirrhosis?" "How can I deal with the death of my uncle, who sexually abused me?" Once we saw that our specific questions would not be answered immediately, they eventually quieted.

The daily schedule for the workshop included several hours of group work consisting of experiential role-play and psychodrama. We also attended a lecture on a different topic each day. The curriculum was focused on our "family of origin" (the family in which we grew up). It was aimed at helping us discover why we are who we are, with a large part of that identity nested in our unique childhoods. At times, many of us became frustrated with the course and complained that we weren't addressing the issues that brought us to the retreat in the first place. Our leaders dismissed our complaints and requested that we remain focused on the curriculum by saying, "If that question persists, we will address it on the last day of the course."

At first, I thought the avoidance of our questions was a therapeutic gimmick ("I'm glad you addressed that. You can think about that this week, and we'll discuss it next time"). Yet the work proved rich, and we settled in. We started appreciating the depth of emotion that the activities created within the group. Still, we were excited about the final day, which promised answers to our questions.

After spending eight hours a day for five days in role-plays focused on the family we grew up in and the relationships within that family, we finally arrived at the last day of our retreat. The group leader explained that we would each have the opportunity to address "one pressing question." She then led us in a role-play, with other group members participating. She might ask a peer to play the role of our "inner child," whispering things we had forgotten about or neglected in ourselves. Our tightly knit group had so grown familiar with each other's issues that we were able to contribute in such a way. Over the course of the past week, we had sat in a sort of theater and watched the history of each other's lives play out. We undertook the roles of child, parent, grandparent, spouse, or sibling for one another.

As we sat together, we came to know each other and ourselves better than we had six days before. Not everything was healed or resolved, but we were able to recognize the origins of our issues. This self-knowledge offered us the ability to forgive ourselves. "Of course you put a lot of weight on what others think of you," they told me after we had acted out some role-plays from my early years. "That is how you survived childhood."

Along with forgiveness came the invitation to move on. "That old context is over," they told me. "You don't have to sacrifice yourself and your own needs anymore so that your single mother struggling with depression will be okay. You can still be loved if you take care of yourself."

Near the end of that final day, as each member presented his or her question, the group leaders set up a quick staging for the role-play. The first group member started with the question, "How do I deal with my alcoholic husband?" From there, the group leader encouraged her to answer questions like "How do you feel?" and "What do you want?" Then the group member was encouraged to find their truth and speak it, regardless of the reaction from the other character being portrayed. Often, the group leader would help guide the other characters involved in the role-play to challenge the group member with arguments, attacks, guilt trips, and other psychological snares. Each member was bolstered in his or her role-play by the wisdom he or she had gained throughout the week about who he or she was. Given that perspective, all of the participants were able to both assert themselves and express what they wanted with clarity and courage.

As it drew closer to being my turn, it dawned on me that I already knew what I needed to do, and that the answer had been there all along. I had been hiding the answer behind the needs, wants, and expectations of others because I had learned when I was young that this was what I had to do in order to survive. I had always been praised for my insight, intellect, and for so capably attending to the needs of others. This was how I managed in a family with a single mother who struggled with low self-esteem and loneliness. I was terrified that she wouldn't make it, and that my family wouldn't make it. The situation required that I grow up quickly, and in having to care for others I neglected caring for myself in order to help my family survive.

This skill set made me an effective leader, teacher, and counselor. However, it also robbed me of the ability to commit my resources to self-care. It also blocked my ability to recognize what I wanted and how to achieve it. It was not the first time I had ever considered my upbringing and its effect on my current life. But this time, this self-exploration during my week at the seminar made its impact crystal clear.

THE QUESTION IS NOT THE QUESTION

As my turn arrived, it was clear that the surface question was not the right question. The real question was "Who am I, and what do I want?" While that may seem like a simple question, many of us never ask it of ourselves. In our program, this is the mission statement, our cornerstone. If we start with this basic question, then our course of action can be much clearer. That action will require creativity, patience, honesty, and courage, but it will allow us to proceed with more confidence and less anxiety and fear toward accomplishing our goals.

I want to be clear about something: fears do not just disappear into thin air. They don't go away with an "aha" moment. It is, however, enough to know that the fears we developed in childhood are no longer real or relevant. Once we realize that, we can walk straight through our fears and into our new lives.

The lessons I learned at the workshop played out each week in sessions I had with my therapist back home. I would go into each session with a specific complaint or worry. Sometimes the theme of the complaint was familiar and chronic; other times, it was unique to that week's particular situation. My therapist would listen patiently, and afterward I would sometimes ask her advice. She rarely answered directly and would often jest, "Well, since you have come to the top of the mountain to meet me, the wisest of sages, I will now impart my wisdom upon you." This was usually her prelude to asking more questions. She would ask for more details, and afterward she would explain what she heard. Hearing her observations about what I was currently experiencing and how she tied them to common themes, I would find the answer to my question. Through this process, I "found" myself again each week. "It is very difficult to find yourself until you are found by someone else first," she told me. "The root of our self is almost always found through another person. When someone else finds us, we come to find ourselves." Realizing that I had the answer to my initial question inside me helped me understand why and how I had been blocked from finding a solution.

In their book, *Parenting from the Inside Out*, Siegel and Hartzell cite new research on the brain as well as recent parenting studies to explain how greater self-awareness in the parents can lead to healthier attachments and healthier developments in children.

> Research in the field of child development has demonstrated that a child's security of attachment to parents is very strongly connected to the parents' understanding of their own early-life experiences .... As a parent, making sense of your life is important

because it supports your ability to provide emotionally connecting and flexible relationships with your children.

They explain that healthy parenting does not hinge on having grown up in a healthy family. Rather, the ability to make sense of and understand oneself demonstrates a certain kind of executive function in the brain that can lead to healthier parenting. The authors issue the edict for parents—to do their own work in order to develop a better understanding of themselves. In so doing, they can provide their children with a healthier context for growing up.

We learn to understand different parts of ourselves—feelings, fears, old scripts, external voices, guilt, imperatives, social pressures—and as we come to know ourselves, we learn to strip away all of the noise that interferes with the essential truth inside of ourselves. As a parent, the more we can strip away all that stuff that blurs our vision, the more clearly we can understand our children and their needs. From there, it is a matter of working through our fears or anxieties and developing some simple skills for communication or setting boundaries. While this process may sound simple, it is painfully difficult.

This premise suggests that we start by looking at the relationship we have with ourselves.

DON'T TRUST EXPERTS— BECOME ONE YOURSELF

Early in my career, I was tempted to pat myself on the back because I thought that I had discovered the secret to good parenting tactics, and that my clients were lucky to have found me. I soon realized that this wasn't the point at all. If clients were presented a solution to all their problems on a silver platter, then they would become dependent on whatever guru was sitting in front of them, whether it be their therapist, a new book on parenting, or a TV or radio host doling out wisdom.

Furthermore, the parent would then constantly feel compelled to consult with experts before making any decision regarding their children.

I soon realized that dispensing advice is not the most effective model for encouraging effective parenting. It's unsustainable, and it doesn't perpetuate growth in the client. My therapist never gave me direct advice, even when I pleaded for it. If she had, I could blame her when it failed or caused me difficulty. Indeed, I have heard parents blame other therapists, experts, programs, and, yes, me for their lack of success in parenting. Let me be clear: *Therapists are not experts on your life. Rather, their expertise is in creating the "container" or experience in which you can discover your truth.* An effective container is a place where one feels safe to explore all the parts of themselves free from judgments—in this way the container is the mind of the therapist. Ideally for children, it is the mind of the parent. The cycle of "ask the expert, get the advice, follow the advice, and blame the expert" removes any ownership by the parents for the results. In addition, parents often complained about divergent expert opinions contributing to their own lack of clarity, hope, and confidence. The key in this equation is that *you* have to make your own choices, and then *own* them.

My goal with this book is not to dole out parenting advice but rather to teach you how to think about the questions you have in raising your children. Only then can you find the truths hidden inside of you.

This process begins with "knowing thyself." Learning how to know yourself is the essence of therapy. I often describe this process as reaching into the chest of a client, making a connection with his insides, and showing them to him. "This is you. This is who you are." Similar to Michelangelo's description of sculpting, "Every block of stone has a statue inside it and it is the task of the sculptor to discover it," this new paradigm is toward enlightenment, a destructive process that asks you to discard all the *shoulds* and untruths that prevent you from knowing what to do.

The task of finding and knowing yourself is a lifelong pursuit. We tend to lose ourselves constantly as we encounter the myriad voices in the world. Some time ago, I was having a conversation with my son during his freshman year in college. "I still have a long way to go before I know myself as well as the average college freshman," I mused. "But can we ever know ourselves, really?" my son wisely replied. This process of self-awareness and self-uncovering is a journey—a lifelong journey.

The starting point of the journey might be revealed in a simple answer to this proverbial therapist's inquiry: "How do you feel?" To parents, examining what *they* feel often seems like a detour in the progress of parenting. Years ago, I worked with a father who described a strong reaction he had to his son's behavior. I asked him how he had felt upon discovering his son's theft. "It is not about a feeling," he shot back. "I feel nothing. He did the wrong thing, and I was just teaching him a lesson by creating this powerful consequence." Clearly, this father *had* experienced a strong feeling, but his anger, embarrassment, fear, or a feeling of powerlessness affected his clarity. It prevented him from clearly seeing his son's needs, feelings, and motives. Without seeing the essence of this situation—without really seeing his son—the likelihood of making a healthy parenting decision was small. This father's inability to identify or clarify his feelings left him without a sense of what his own motives might be. Maybe he saw his son as an extension of himself, and the theft represented a threat to his own sense of adequacy as a parent. From this standpoint, his motive would be based on his needs rather than needs of his son.

Stephen A. Mitchell, in his book *Influence and Autonomy in Psychoanalysis,* offers insight into the difference between adhering to an ideology, theory, or set of techniques versus learning how to think about the practice of analysis. Rather than subscribing to dogma, he suggests that the practice requires a "special kind of experience and thinking." We can adapt his ideas here and apply them to learning how to think about parenting:

The emphasis is not on behaviors but on rigorous thinking, not on constraints but on self-reflective emotional involvement, not on the application of general truths but on imaginative participation. This suggests a very different sort of technique. The discipline is not in the procedures, but in the sensibility through which the analyst participates . . . there is no generic solution or technique. There is a great deal of disciplined thought in the skilled practice of clinical psychoanalysis, and continual, complex choices.

If we apply this idea to parenting, the central task in parenting becomes learning how to feel and how to think.

The following chapters will explore parenting principles and the questions that many parents have about them. I will explore thoughts and principles embedded within each question. The focus will not be the content of the question itself, but rather the *thinking* that goes into answering it. In my work, I often respond to parents' questions or decisions with these words in mind: "I don't really know what you should decide. There may not be a 'right answer' or there may be many 'right' answers. But I will ask you to challenge how you came to your conclusion. I will challenge the 'why' of your choice but not the 'what' of your decision."

My aim is to help parents become more intentional. As parents learn to ask deeper questions, answers begin to flow more naturally. Once again, it's important to remember that this practice will be a lifelong journey.

Joseph Campbell, the renowned philosopher and scholar, observed that the world's myths share a core pattern, which he called "the Hero's Journey." It describes the plight of humankind and can be found in epic stories, religions, and the lives of every person. There are three major chapters in this journey: the separation, the initiation, and the return. First, in order to enter the stage of separation, the hero must heed the call to adventure. He must leave what he knows and travel into the darkness of the unknown to undergo his own personal quest. This journey provides him with lessons he needs in *his* life. Raising children struggling with mental health issues, addictions, or even the normal angst of growing up can be scary and confusing for a parent. We are asked to look into the dark places within ourselves, and confront and make peace with our fears. We are asked to let go of what has made us feel safe and secure and embrace some things that may cause us pain. Our children are not the only ones experiencing initiation; at times they provide the call for instigating the whole family's journey down this road. A profound aspect of this journey is that the call to adventure is often initially refused. This refusal applies to both the child or parent, as they experience a parallel process. I hope as you answer the call that this book might serve as a tool for you on your journey to find the answers hidden inside of you.

3•24•18 -
Confronted J about his being active in his addiction currently. The choices he continues to make are unacceptable to me. I do feel it is just too late to even try to reconcile a marriage. Especially since its been over for so many years already. He is still trying to put it back on me and point the finger back at me and he's still defensive.
Josie just got back from J.T. At first it was a loving return then she's probably just tired. now she's still a bit distant. Her friend is over. I think she might be mad at me for sending her dad away again.

CHAPTER TWO

ENLIGHTENED AND INTENTIONAL PARENTING

More important than the question of what to do is why.

OFTEN, DURING MY LECTURES OR BROADCASTS, A PARent will ask me simple questions such as "Should I ground my son for staying out fifteen minutes late?" "What is a good consequence for lying?" "Should I allow my seventeen-year-old daughter who is recovering from drugs to smoke cigarettes?" "How much should I monitor my son's friends? Is it okay to put spyware on his computer or phone?" "Should I tell my child I am disappointed or proud?" My response will likely be a series of questions and stories that serve to illustrate the principles involved in addressing their inquiries. Parents will often try to steer me toward a specific and concrete answer to their question; instead I offer them a way to think about the question so that they might discover the answer for themselves.

One summer I was working with a young man dealing with a serious addiction. He and his family had been through several treatment programs before enrolling him in our wilderness program. There had been some temporary success, but inevitably he would relapse. The situation was critical, and the young man's life hung in the balance.

While the parents had been introduced to Al-Anon, I believed there was a lack of focus on their own recovery. Our first few phone calls exposed their anxiety, which was real and earned. As I began to shift the focus from what they couldn't control to what they could control—centering on their *own* recovery versus their son's recovery—we began to see progress. During one call, after reviewing their son's letters full of despair, shame, and sadness, the father asked me, "If I write and tell him I love him, will he—" He stopped and started again. "I just want to write so he will—" He started like this a few times and then finally said, "It is hard to know what to say when I let go of the outcome, when I let go of the idea that I can control how he feels. When I stop thinking about his reaction, I don't know what to say."

This revelation gets to the heart of the very spirit of enlightened and intentional parenting. This father had lost his own truth. He had lost it because he had had become too focused on his son's reaction. He had become obsessed and believed that he could control his son and his addiction, even his sense of hope. In the end, he had come to engage his son and his son's addiction in a power struggle. Finally, this father was learning how to think about his own parenting decisions. He was learning to ask himself about his intent.

During a recent parent lecture, I was addressing assertive communication and behavioral change and stated that we ought to avoid using our feelings as tools to guilt our children into changing. One mother responded, "But can't we share our feelings of disappointment or sadness with our children?" Before I could answer, another mother in the crowd asked, "Why? Why do you want to share those feelings with your child?"

The first mother paused thoughtfully, then said tentatively, "Because it's the truth?" And, after another pause, "Because I want him to stop doing the things that I am worried about." Eureka! That's it! We can begin to answer our own questions about parenting once we learn to ask ourselves the deeper questions: What is our truth? What is our intention? What is our primary goal? Is there a skill set we need to learn or improve upon that will help us to be more clear and efficient in communicating with or relating to our children? Are we saying what we mean and meaning what we say? Do we see ourselves clearly, and subsequently see our children and their needs clearly? Are we separating our needs from their needs and addressing them separately?

I have a business associate who occasionally helps me get clarity in order to better understand my intentions and my course of action. I call him my muse. My therapist, my wife, and a few colleagues also help me in this capacity. The process looks like this: I present a question or a dilemma, and through a series of questions from him, my truth becomes clear. Just hearing myself describe the situation brings clarity. I am able to get clear on my intentions once they are stripped of any hidden agendas and freed from all the noise, voices, and potential reactions that others might have. It doesn't matter if it is a business decision, a parenting issue, or another relationship concern; the principle is always the same.

The clarity I gain in thinking through a problem doesn't remove my fears and anxieties, but it does put them into perspective. I regularly experience this in my own therapy sessions. In each session I find myself again, and then am faced with the task of going into the world and staying true to myself. My fear doesn't disappear, but it does become more manageable. I can face it because who I am is okay.

These are the principles of enlightened and intentional parenting: learning how to think about the questions we have as parents in a new way, learning how to connect, understanding our children, and removing any obstacles that obscure our clarity. The lessons herein equip us with the tools we need to find our own truth—and thus to be free and clear to find our children. This model of parenting will offer peace, hope, and a sense of empowerment.

TEACHING CHILDREN TO FEEL

When I signed up to be a therapist, I thought it was my job to make people happy. I was good at listening, offering insight, and presenting my unique perspective to family and friends. I was good at solving problems. I thought these skills served me in being a "healer." Not only was the notion that I was going to fix what others couldn't fix in themselves self-centered and arrogant, it was diametrically off course. Like many of us who enlist in the business of helping people, I was ready to solve the world's problems and rescue people from their pain with my unique gifts.

Then I went to school. Life happened. And I went to therapy.

I realized that my job was not to make people happy but to help people feel sad. My intent is not to inflict injury or cause pain, but to help people to feel. It is my job to help others learn *how* to feel their pain and sadness in order to rid themselves of paralysis in moving forward. (Ironically, I realized that much of the wisdom I had to offer people was forged from the pain I felt growing up.) It was not my job to take away a person's chance to learn and find meaning in their suffering. Viktor Frankl wrote in his harrowing memoir of Auschwitz that trying to find happiness was the sure path to meaninglessness and unhappiness. Rather, it is our task to give our suffering meaning and learn from it—this process ascribes value to it. As Thich Nhat Hanh explains,

> Many people aspire to go to a place where pain and suffering do not exist, a place where there is only happiness. This is a rather dangerous idea, for compassion is not possible without pain and suffering. It is only when we enter into contact with suffering that understanding and compassion can be born. Without suffering, we do not have the opportunity to cultivate compassion and understanding; and without understanding, there can be no true love.

I can think of many examples of working with people where my impulse was to give them a "look on the bright side" story or "reframe" a difficult situation to bring them to a happier, more peaceful place. This tactic is often reinforced by the person's relief from his pain, but it misses the essence that a life fully lived will involve some suffering. Eventually, I came to believe it was my job to help people authentically suffer so that they could heal. Carl Jung explains, "Neurosis is a substitute form of legitimate suffering."

One rainy day in the wilderness of Utah, something happened that crystallized this idea of authentic suffering. I was sitting on the log of an old broken-down fence with one of my students. Adam had experienced a difficult morning. He had some problems with peers in his group; they had been bickering over chores, which eventually led to Adam earning a time-out from the group to calm down and reflect. I had the notion that part of what was going on with Adam had nothing to do with his fellow group members and the chores he had been assigned, but rather something from outside his wilderness experience. Something else was nagging at him, pulling at him, hurting him. The arguments with his peers were a detour, a distraction.

So I sat with Adam and asked him how he was doing. There were long pauses and moments of silence as I waited for him to speak. Eventually, through quiet sobs, he started to talk about his mother. She had died a few years earlier and his father was raising him alone. Despite deep love for his son, his father often did not "get" Adam. He didn't connect with Adam like his mother had. Adam's wound was intense and primal. The disagreements with his peers echoed feelings of isolation and alienation he had felt in the absence of his mother. In the wet and quiet space, Adam poured out his loss, aching for his mother and wishing that she were still in his life, wishing she were there that day, wishing he could write her, wishing he could look forward to seeing her at the conclusion of his program, wishing he could hug her and share his progress with her.

As the lump in my throat began to grow and tears filled my eyes, I realized I didn't have anything to offer Adam in the way of "Look on the bright side" or "Let's look at this differently. Let me help you see this loss as something positive." I felt utterly powerless. What could I say or do to help Adam? I had no answers for him, no way to bring his mother back to him, no way to talk him out of his pain. I had been working with Adam to discover his anger and pain, and suddenly it was spilling out in the rain, near this broken fence, with me. What a disservice it would have been to him if I had tried to take that authentic suffering away. The only thing I had to offer was myself, sitting there *with* him, crying *with* him in the rain.

Therapists call this "containment." Parents call it "unbearable." Yet containment gives our children a sense that they are okay. As therapists and parents, we must challenge ourselves. We mustn't let our desire to alleviate Adam's pain—to avoid our own empathic misery—interfere with Adam's need to feel, hurt, grieve, suffer, love, and survive. I had to put aside my instinct to rescue Adam from his difficult emotions, help him not feel "bad" or sad only to selfishly rescue myself from feeling bad.

Deep down, it is at the very core of our nature to want to help someone feel better when they are suffering, to take it away. Yet in this instance, the most amazing thing happened. In the midst of absolute impotence, I realized that I felt utterly connected to Adam. What I knew I had to do in that moment was to put my arm around him while we sat side by side on that fence, in the rain. I told him that I was there with him and that I was so sorry that he had lost his mother; I felt his pain and suffering alongside him. We cried for a long while together. We felt powerless and sad, and entirely connected.

Whenever I think about what it is to be a therapist, parent, adult, listener, or confidant in somebody's life, I am reminded of Adam's story. I think about how we can't offer anybody happiness, nor is it our job to *make* people happy. It is, however, our job to offer love, to offer the intimacy of our companionship when someone we care about suffers. This is what it means to *truly* be there for someone, to be in someone's life, to be truly intimate and connected with him in meaningful ways.

So in order to help our children and others learn to negotiate, manage, and ultimately heal, we can offer them our vulnerable selves. In fact, their healing starts with self-love that often grows from being found and loved, and leads to the ability to overcome life's challenges. This is a crucial ingredient in building resiliency.

> *As parents, we need to allow our children to actually feel their emotions, to deeply experience their experiences, and be there for them in intimate ways as they struggle.*

This authenticity and connection is a key contribution to resiliency in our children. Therefore, it is critical for parents to learn how to allow their children to authentically suffer and manage difficult emotions, to be there with them in ways that will be connected, and to help them avoid anesthetizing themselves from their pain and from the consequences of their behavior. Teaching children to feel also creates the ability for them to recognize emotion in others, thus increasing the capacity for empathy.

NO ONE RIGHT WAY TO RAISE A CHILD

Within the pages of this book, you will discover some of the secrets of being a "good parent" and the coincidence of raising good children. You will learn to focus on the *process* of parenting. You will learn to focus on what you can control, and experience the liberation and optimism that comes with letting go of what you can't control. You will learn to focus on your own recovery and parenting skills, and in doing so you will gain the reward of inner strength, confidence, peace, and efficacy—even in the presence of the everyday struggle of raising children. The scope of this book is about parenting with power, intimacy, and connection—I call this "empowered parenting." Additionally, the principles in this book will be applicable to virtually every relationship in your life.

Because it is impossible to tell you how to raise your individual child, or how to speak to each child's specific personality or each parent's particular situation, a basic theoretical understanding of the principles is needed. This will create a foundation for the subsequent tools that will be discussed. With this foundation, you will be armed with the ability to apply these skills in varied contexts unique to your child and to his or her individual personality and situation. Without this foundation the tools could be misused, misunderstood, or used outside of a healthy context. After all, a hammer is useful, but has little value without a plan or an understanding of that blueprint. In fact, a hammer can be used to harm or destroy; it only has value in relationship to the appropriate goals.

This is where most parenting books fail. There is not one "right" way to raise a child; there are a million "right" ways to raise a child. Furthermore, there is no one way, one skill, or one parenting technique that will be definitive in terms of its "rightness." If that is not enough to catch your attention, there is also no way you are going to avoid screwing up as a parent. You *will* make mistakes, even, at times, big ones.

My message may not be compelling for the average person, but it is a reality. If you have experienced the pain of watching your child stand on the edge of a building, literally or metaphorically, considering jumping; if the pain of raising a child who struggles has cracked your heart open to search for answers; if you have listened to professionals and friends offer advice with assurances that if you do it "right" your child will be okay . . . . If you are that person, then what I write will speak to you. Like taking a breath after being underwater to the point of desperation, the redirection toward finding your truth will provide relief from the suffocation of fear and anxiety. What I write will lead you away from quick-fix advice and simple solutions; instead, it offers you a type of peace that allows you to quiet all the "expert voices" that cloud your wisdom buried beneath self-doubt. This book is about finding your center. It doesn't promise that everything will be okay if you do what I say, but it promises that you will be okay if you accept the invitation to make your own serenity your lifelong project. I don't know what is best for you or your child—you do. And if I give you tools or techniques with the promise that you can help your child avoid mistakes, detours, and pain, then I am fundamentally off course.

Sometimes parents listen to a lecture of mine or have a conversation with me where they conclude to follow a certain course. Then, around the corner, some of the details of the situation change and they become disoriented, asking for more direction. I want you to stretch, really reach for your inner wisdom. I want to provide you tools to make contact with the light that is hidden beneath trauma and judgments that cause you confusion. A Buddhist master was once asked about his dogma and responded, "We don't have dogma. We dance." This way of teaching invites you to understand a way of being in the world. And when we understand the way, everything begins to make sense. This is the journey of the heroic parent.

Jeffrey just called me on the phone from his dads still saying that circumstantial hard time and problems caused his alcoholism. This is why I have no choice, if I want to stay true to myself, but to divorce him.

CHAPTER THREE

A MODEL FOR UNDERSTANDING YOUR CHILD

I could hear my mother say I've fallen to the world
and its filthy way,
Drowning in a puddle of sin, but my heart's this way.
I'm sorry for the mess that I made,
If you could open up your ears you could hear what
I have to say,
I could pour it, I could leave it on your table for days.

—lyrics by Kyle Henderson

BEFORE RUSHING TO TRY TO CHANGE A CHILD'S BEHAVIOR, it is crucial to take time to understand what that behavior might be telling us. In fact, in the process of understanding behavior, the person suffering from the malady, the child, can often find her own solution. That is because the behavior likely served her in some other context that may no longer exist. A teenager may promise her parents that she'll change, that the bad behavior won't happen again, but she may miss an opportunity to discover the core issue that led to the behavior in the first place. In such cases I ask the family to slow down, as it is valuable for us to understand what is going on under the surface in order to effect change. The process of simple behavior management is not healing, but it is akin to treating the symptoms without understanding their root causes. In this kind of a "cutting the weed off at the surface," we will see symptoms crop up in other areas of our lives. Symptoms are evidence of wounds and to adequately heal those wounds we must clearly understand them. Dr. Jami Gill illustrates this beautifully in her book *Finding Human*: "The point of the quest, again and again, is to replace perfection with completeness. That which is excluded must become your enemy and defeat you."

Most often when a new therapist calls me for a consult with one of their cases, I find that the challenge is that they see the parent as an obstacle to the child's healing. I will often ask them to understand that the parent is a client too. "What would you say if the parent were your client? Would you be angry and frustrated with them? Or would you hold them with love and try to help them heal? When you get frustrated with the parent, you have lost contact with them." When the therapist is reminded that parents have wounds too and that those wounds are the origin of their problems, they immediately respond to the parent in healing ways.

The following image, which represents a concept known as the cycle of health and wholeness, illustrates what I and many other therapists believe about surface symptoms and the root issues they often obscure. I have found this model to be helpful for both parents and children in outlining the relationship we have with our feelings and emotions.

In the illustration, the cycle of health and wholeness appears to have a beginning and end. But in reality, the cycle represents the ongoing, lifelong journey as well as the journey we experience on a daily basis.

The Cycle of Health and Wholeness

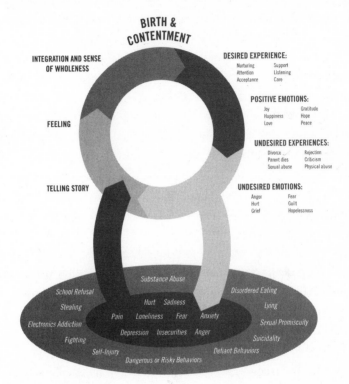

BIRTH &
CONTENTMENT

INTEGRATION AND SENSE
OF WHOLENESS

DESIRED EXPERIENCE:
Nurturing   Support
Attention   Listening
Acceptance   Care

POSITIVE EMOTIONS:
Joy   Gratitude
Happiness   Hope
Love   Peace

FEELING

UNDESIRED EXPERIENCES:
Divorce   Rejection
Parent dies   Criticism
Sexual abuse Physical abuse

TELLING STORY

UNDESIRED EMOTIONS:
Anger   Fear
Hurt   Guilt
Grief   Hopelessness

Substance Abuse
School Refusal   Disordered Eating
Stealing   Hurt   Sadness   Lying
Pain   Loneliness Fear   Anxiety
Electronics Addiction   Sexual Promiscuity
Depression Insecurities Anger
Fighting   Suicidality
Self-Injury   Defiant Behaviors
Dangerous or Risky Behaviors

CONTENTMENT

Our children are content only when they are at peace emotionally, spiritually, physically, and mentally. Contentment is, at some level, the state of being to which all human beings strive. But it is rare that we feel contentment in all areas of our lives at the same time. We may feel contentment at work when we accomplish a pressing task, solve a certain problem, make a sale, finish a project, or win a case. We may also experience contentment when we resolve a conflict with our spouse, or when we see our son or daughter achieve a goal.

My desire is to help you be a model of contentment for your children, to show you how to embody an overall state of well-being, even when you are experiencing challenges in specific areas of your life. In doing so, you will achieve a better sense of happiness, but you will also help your children develop the necessary tools and skills they need to find their own path of contentment.

Be warned, however, that you cannot force contentment on anyone—you cannot install it in someone like software on a computer. As much as you may strive, desire, or even ache to do so, you cannot force your children to be content. In my experience, I've found that the more parents attempt to force contentment onto their children—even those with the most benevolent desires—they invariably elicit a fight for the right to feel.

It is natural for children to want to push for their independence from your control. This is a normal aspect of them developing their identities. If you try to force your version of contentment on them, you'll only give your children another obstacle to overcome in seeking and finding their own happiness: the obstacle of you and *your* issues. In short, no matter how much you want contentment for your children, they have to find it for themselves.

Your children deserve the right to feel what they feel.

NEEDS AND DESIRED EMOTIONS

We are born into this life as fairly helpless creatures, dependent on our caregivers to meet our needs. These needs include keeping us warm (but not too warm), dry, fed, hydrated, clean, stimulated (but not too stimulated), rested, and, hopefully, free from disease. Infants are demanding, and it takes a lot of time and energy to be a parent. We invest our financial, psychological, and emotional resources in caring for an infant.

As parents, we want to provide more than the basics of food, water, and shelter for our children; we want them to be educated, successful in their relationships and careers—even more so than we were—and we want them to grow up to be happy.

As a wilderness therapist, I ask parents to brainstorm a list of basic human needs. First, they invariably offer basic things such as food, water, shelter, air, and warmth. Then they typically enhance the list with deeper human needs such as love, acceptance, belonging, trust, honesty, spirituality, self-esteem, connectedness, and intimacy.

You can certainly find plenty of examples to illustrate that love and relationships are essential to life. There are studies of infants who receive adequate nutrition but fail to develop at normal rates because they were provided insufficient connection to caregivers. Psychologist Harry Harlow's experiments showed that monkeys who were raised without a warm and caring surrogate developed digestive difficulties. He also observed that monkeys who were in the presence of a surrogate had less of a fear response when exposed to startling stimuli. His experiments demonstrated that for young monkeys, the proper amount of food and physiological support was not the sole predictor of physical health and resilience. As with human babies, love and connection were necessary.

The movie *Cast Away* with Tom Hanks depicts the adult version of this need. In the fictionalized story, a man with a relatively stable and successful life is marooned on a deserted island. With considerable effort, he is able to provide himself with the basic needs of food, water, shelter, and warmth. What his meager existence lacks is human interaction.

The character in the movie does what he can to create a purpose for his life. He keeps a FedEx package, determined to deliver it to its recipient; he clings to the idea of returning to his family. These goals give his suffering meaning and value. Devoid of human contact for several years, Hanks' character creates a friendship with an inanimate object—a volleyball he names Wilson—to fulfill his basic need for relationships and human connection. Unlike an infant, he already had a history of significant human connection in his life. However, he becomes despondent about the unlikelihood of having future connections, and even considers suicide.

We are, by our very nature, relationally based creatures. We need human contact, love, and acceptance to feel healthy and whole. Some of us have more need and desire for connectedness than others, but we all have these instincts. When we have our needs met, we experience desired emotions such as love, trust, belongingness, and connectedness. This is the aforementioned state of contentment, in which we feel good, happy, peaceful, and successful. Contentment happens when we feel valued, connected, and loved. This is what makes life worth living; this is what drives us to thrive as infants, children, adolescents, and as adults. We want these feelings for our children and ourselves.

UNMET NEEDS AND UNDESIRED EMOTIONS

Just as love, affection, and connection bring us desired emotions that we can loosely define as contentment, the opposite is also true. When we lack love, affection, and connection, we feel undesired emotions such as loneliness, sadness, and neglect, which produce *discontentment*. We can also experience pain and trauma through experiences such as the loss of a loved one, divorce, abuse, rejection by friends, or failure at work or school.

In my parenting workshops, when we work on the list of needs, I also pose the questions, "What about *pain*? Is pain a human need?" A lively discussion often ensues. Some argue that we do not need pain in the same way we need love or affection. Many parents are initially resistant to the idea of pain as a human need—until they start to consider it more fully.

In the book *Pain: The Gift Nobody Wants*, Brand and Yancy tell the story of a child who is born with a rare neurological disorder through which she is literally unable to feel physical pain. As the girl grows and begins to interact with her environment, she injures herself repeatedly but remains completely unaware that anything has occurred. Minor injuries go unnoticed until they become major problems; sprained ankles turn into damaged tissue and ligaments, cuts and bruises turn into abscesses and infections. By age eleven, she has lost most of her fingers, suffers from multiple skin and tongue ulcers, and has to have both of her legs amputated due to complications from self-inflicted injuries. Crippled with all these ailments, the young girl is a powerful symbol of a life without pain.

We can conclude from this example that pain serves an essential, though uncomfortable, role in our lives. It operates as a survival mechanism, instructing us in the physical, emotional, psychological, and spiritual aspects of our existence. We may also conclude that pain is a counterbalance to happiness and contentment, and that we may not fully appreciate one without the other.

The final truth about pain is that it is indifferent. Pain neither respects nor discriminates, it is part of the human condition, something every one of us experiences. Whether it is physical, spiritual, mental, psychological, or emotional, pain is inevitable.

All of the great souls on earth have felt deep pain for themselves as well as the empathic pain that love asks of us. The problem is not in the feeling of pain but in our *relationship to pain*. How we respond to and think about our pain will determine whether we return to contentment or sink into further suffering. When we understand that our pain is our love uncovered, that feeling pain means that we are alive, we move away from behaviors that anesthetize us and embrace our pain as part of a life that is whole.

As a parent, we will feel pain.

EMOTIONAL BLOCKS
AND ATTEMPTED SOLUTIONS

Just as when we touch a hot stove and immediately pull back our hand, when we experience pain in any area of our lives, we tend to react in self-protective ways. We take action to alleviate, stop, or avoid it. Research indicates humans are much more likely to act to avoid pain, fear, and undesired outcomes than we are to act to achieve desired goals.

My experience has shown that through the healthy experiencing of pain, one is able to develop a sense of contentment through integration; conversely, it is precisely through the avoidance of pain that the greatest suffering occurs.

I want to help you feel your pain more purely, and to experience it without it overwhelming you. This will provide you with opportunities to help your children develop healthy coping mechanisms as they navigate pain in their own lives. As you learn to recognize the uncomfortable emotions that arise when you are evaluating your children's pain, you can respond by intimately connecting with them.

Today's culture bombards both parents and children with messages about anesthetizing pain and discontentment. Television programs show parents telling their children, "Don't feel bad." Pharmaceutical companies aggressively market medications designed to "solve" depression, anxiety, weight loss, and erectile dysfunction, among many others. Pain relievers are marketed for specific conditions such as migraines, joint and muscle pain, arthritis, and tension headaches. Advertisers sing a siren song for a pain-free life.

As a society, we sometimes behave as if suffering is contagious. If we can't help relieve pain in other people, maybe we can protect ourselves by avoiding them. Those who have experienced chronic illnesses or unthinkable tragedy in their families often attest that only a few brave souls tread the painful path with them, and that even those people struggled to stay present with them through their pain. Likewise, when a coworker or friend struggles, it is our natural response to want to cheer them up. We want to distract them from their pain and assure them everything will soon be okay.

We act as though avoiding pain will lead to a more joyful life, but I assert that feeling pain shows us that we are alive. Your pain will lead you to where you love, where you need, and where you feel joy. To eliminate or run away from it leads to addiction, emptiness, and meaninglessness.

To truly support someone, you must walk the path of difficulty with them. You must hurt with them, and acknowledge your powerlessness over their pain.

To suffer along with someone is an experience not many seek or cultivate. Sharing suffering, particularly with a child, brings up difficult emotions within ourselves, causing us to experience our own discomfort and pain. Therefore, we tend to react in protective ways to circumvent that discomfort and avoid others' suffering. As parents watching our children suffer, we may react defensively to their pain because we make the incorrect assumption that their suffering is our fault. We may respond by shaming them for being hurt, or by trying to distract or rescue them so that we, as parents, can feel absolved.

COPING MECHANISMS

As we progress through life, we learn several ways to deal with uncomfortable emotions and discontentment. These coping mechanisms can be overtly or covertly taught by our families. Some others are taught to us by our friends and acquaintances, some we learn from our culture, and still others we devise on our own.

Not all coping mechanisms are counterproductive, of course. Some are effective in helping us move through difficult emotions and toward facing the root issue. Still, a lot of our coping mechanisms can be unhealthy. Instead of encouraging us to deal with the problem, they can distract, gloss over, and take energy away from us. Our dysfunctional coping mechanisms are analogous to taking Percocet for a headache that is caused by a brain tumor. The pill may offer relief from the pain, but it fails to address its origin. If we take the analogy further, the Percocet, in this instance, temporarily resolves the pain, and placates the patient so that he does not seek further evaluation of the problem, even though tests could lead to discovery and perhaps a cure. Such action leaves the root cause—in this case perhaps, a brain tumor—undiagnosed, which in the end may result in increased complications from a lack of appropriate treatment, and perhaps even, eventually, death. So it is with unhealthy coping mechanisms. If we ignore or medicate to dull pain and discontentment, we may allow a serious condition to go undiscovered, unexamined, and, therefore, untreated.

Let's go back to the cycle of health and wholeness (on pg. 23), which promotes the idea that we all have needs. When those needs are met, we are more or less content; when they are not met, we experience discontentment. We have already discussed the necessity of pain. Now, I ask you: How do we, as human beings, typically attempt to manage our pain? When I ask this question in parent seminars, parents are quick to develop a laundry list of behaviors in which their *children* engage— prescription and illegal drug abuse, alcohol abuse, acting out sexually, running away from home, eating disorders, lying, stealing, truancy problems, dropping out of school, pornography, computer addiction, withdrawal, aggression, defiance, excessive exercise....

At this point I say to parents, "You answered with behaviors that your sons or daughters have been using to cope with *their* pain, but I was intentional when I asked, 'How do *we*, as human beings, attempt to manage our pain?'" Many then have an "aha" moment and realize that a lot of what their son or daughter has been doing to manage his or her own stress and pain is similar or complementary—although perhaps different in degree and magnitude—to their own coping styles and mechanisms.

It is difficult for some parents to examine themselves and their own coping mechanisms when they look at their children's struggles. They often don't notice that their own dysfunctional coping mechanisms may actually be part of the problem their child is experiencing.

The tendency for parents to focus on their child's problems instead of their own also reveals a fundamental block in effectively addressing the situation. In general, it is easier to recognize problems in others because it is less painful than seeing the issues within ourselves. Focusing on the problems of another person, however, leads to disempowerment. We become the victim of the problem, and because that problem is in another person, our happiness becomes dependent on *their* changing. I have come to realize in

Parents may distract themselves from their own pain and discontentment by overfocusing on the needs of their struggling child and underfocusing on their own needs.

my own therapy and in working with a large number of parents that if we focus on what we can't control, we'll inevitably suffer from anxieties and depression. Whereas if we focus on what is within our control, no matter how daunting, we will be less likely to suffer from such debilitating feelings. Even though the challenges of self-growth can be immense, just the realization alone that our problems reside within ourselves can generate a sense of liberation and empowerment.

This focus on the self also reorients the relationship we have with our children. When we make our own happiness our lifelong project, we model a healthy vulnerability for them. And by steering clear of trying to control someone else, in this case our children, we avoid teaching them that our happiness is their responsibility—a burden they may try to carry out of a sense of filial obligation but ultimately cannot bear. With this focus on self, we often become more effective at influencing and encouraging change in our children.

ATTEMPTED SOLUTIONS

The premise of attempted solutions is simply this: virtually every symptom we experience is our best attempt to alleviate our suffering. This nonjudgmental way of understanding symptoms sees them as an attempt to cope with undesirable feelings. Even when they seem irrational or absurd, our symptoms serve to alleviate our suffering in some capacity. Parents often react intensely to their child's symptoms, and their reactions stem from love and concern for their child. However, the sadness, anger, and frustration they feel may be interpreted consciously or unconsciously by the child as a judgment: "You are wrong or bad for feeling these feelings." "You are causing your father and mother pain." "You should have a strong sense of guilt, shame, and regret for your behaviors." This perception (or misperception) is precisely why it is important that therapists and parents reframe the conversation. Shifting to the pragmatic solution of removing dangerous coping mechanisms, and replacing them with effective, sustainable coping in the form of *feeling*, puts parent and child on the path toward contentment.

Sometimes a parent's response to a child's symptom is a sort of contrived confusion. This is different from the genuine confusion that parents feel when they initially encounter their child's problems. Authentic confusion is clarified by reading, by listening to a therapist describe the dynamic, or by getting other education on the problem. Contrived confusion—repeating "I don't know why she is doing this"—creates a kind of disconnect and shame. This nagging line of questioning suggests to the child, "You are crazy for feeling this way" or "You shouldn't feel this way."

Unhealthy coping causes our children to spiral into their symptoms and develop a style that is referred to as a disorder.

We are all prone to a certain style where it comes to our mental health, and under duress we gravitate toward those themes, like a record player into a groove. Based on a combination of our genetic predispositions and exposure in our environment, such behaviors include anxieties, depression, addictions, obsessions, and compulsions. Such symptoms serve another purpose: they draw attention away from the genuine pain that sometimes seems unbearable. They obscure "authentic suffering" and offer a substitute: a more palatable version of distress. Understanding symptoms in this context can help us to see them for what they are: *indicators of another problem or a wound*, rather than simply problems themselves.

TELLING OUR STORY

"Telling our story" is a general expression that refers to our need to talk about something. Sharing our own personal narrative helps us make sense of it, and if the person with whom we share our story is a capable listener, then we are not alone in it. By telling our story, we re-experience those emotions and "pass through" our pain. And as we pass through our pain, it passes through us.

Often we get stuck on a certain problem because we have not allowed ourselves to pass through the pain. This can sometimes be triggered by present or past relationships, in which we battle instincts to avoid feeling discomfort in order to save ourselves from getting hurt. These messages range from "Get over it," to "You're too sensitive," to more benign examples like "It's not so bad." It can be valuable to just sit with your emotions and allow others to do the same. I have found a lot of success in asking others not to "solve" my emotions (when they see themselves as helping me with my problems), but instead asking if they can tolerate my emotions and me.

The resolution of the cycle of health and wholeness is found within ourselves. This model suggests that through our own resources and strength we can find peace, meaning, and integration. If we are allowed to feel—and especially if someone can be there with us as we feel—then we will be okay. Our wounds will heal. Our losses will soften. Our pain will become a part of our depth, our passion, and our meaning.

So, in the case of our children, part of what parents have to do is to get out of the way. I often say that parents can do more to disrupt this process of integration than they can ever do to facilitate it.

Learn to listen, sit, contain, and just be with your children.

Pack your lectures and your solutions and your analogies away unless your children specifically ask for them, and instead just learn to be present with them. This is what it means to nurture. This is what it means to love and to be a good parent. I have felt no greater joy, intimacy, or connection than when I have been on the listening side of such an exchange—both as a parent and as a therapist. I believe that if we can learn to be with our children in this way, then when they struggle and want help, they will be more likely to approach us for help than to hide their pain away.

THE MISTAKE MANY PARENTS MAKE

Indeed, our society shares a belief that pain is a problem to be avoided, and that the path to happiness is to avoid struggle. Rebecca Armstrong makes the point this way: "Joseph Campbell gave his students graduating from Sarah Lawrence this advice: 'Don't do what Daddy says, because Daddy has one interest in mind for you and that's your security. And if you bargain away your life for security now, you will never find your bliss.'"

Our instinct to comfort and provide safety for our children, while well meaning, can become a barrier to their spiritual and psychological growth if we don't pay close attention.

It is our job as parents to create a safe and nurturing environment for our children, but when that instinct also subconsciously suggests to our children that they ought not to feel something because we find it threatening or unpleasant, then we lose our connection with them. Frustration, anxiety, and judgment are emotions that belong to us as parents, and they are evidence that we have lost contact with the *other*.

During my college studies, we watched a documentary about the life of a Utah mother, and saw how well her typical day was organized. There was a time and place for everything—meals, reading, drawing, naps, music, exercise. She was ostensibly running an intensive pre-school in her home, with her own children. The mother noted that sometimes, when the kids became rambunctious, scheduled physical exercise became necessary for the children. She then redirected the physical spontaneity of the children into structured calisthenics.

When the children napped, this mother cleaned the house, evaluated the day, and continued to refine the children's schedule. When the kids woke from their naps, it was time to continue the curriculum. After bedtime, the mother prepared meals for the coming days, freezing dinners for future use. Meanwhile, the father worked during the day—leaving early and returning in the evening. This family's organized and efficient life was impressive.

We then watched a documentary about a family from a developing country, whose home had few modern comforts. There were specific gender roles, too. The fathers and young men went out to hunt and gather honey together. The young men learned stories, rituals, and legends from their fathers, singing songs that related both to their own spiritual heritage and to survival. Most importantly, they learned from the older men how to hunt and gather food for their and their family's survival.

The women took the younger boys and the female children to fish and take care of the home during the day. They wove baskets and did numerous household tasks. They carried the children on their backs and sang songs containing legends, rituals, allegories, and stories about their culture and way of life.

Both the men and women made children part of their daily routines, naturally attending to their physical, spiritual, emotional, and psychological needs. The parents taught their kids important life lessons in the moment, as instructional situations occurred. Though every day was a struggle to survive, the children learned many of life's most important lessons through that struggle.

Students of many disciplines learn Maslow's hierarchy of needs; it is often interpreted that basic needs for food, water, and shelter must be met before a person can meet higher-level needs such as belonging, self-worth, and identity formation. Viewing the two families in the documentary, it became clear to me that this assertion is wrong. We witnessed a primitive family teaching their children what it meant to belong, what it meant to be who they are, and what it meant to have a basic sense of efficacy and worth—and they did this all naturally, *in the context* of their struggles for survival.

The Utah mother, on the other hand, creates lessons, develops curriculums, and turns spontaneous physicality into a structured exercise experience. She gathers and prepares food outside of its natural context—at best she takes the kids to the grocery store to buy food with money the father earns. She then prepares meals while the children are removed from the process. The father is not present for much of this day, so the children attach neither to his work nor to the experience of his role in providing for the family.

In modern culture, it is difficult to teach children the lessons that come naturally to the more primitive family in this example. In our culture, parents must explicitly teach the lessons of belonging and identity, as well as concepts such as the law of the harvest. A primary principle of wilderness therapy is that we interpret Maslow's hierarchal needs pyramid upside down. Wilderness therapy teaches that within the context of struggling to survive a person learns who he is, what it means to belong, and what it means to be interdependent. Within the wilderness context, one learns values. If you choose not to make a fire, you will be cold and unable to eat a hot meal. If you aren't careful when building your shelter, you will have an uncomfortable night of sleep. In situations like this, truths about preparation, patience, and organization are inescapable.

I remember my first client after becoming a wilderness therapist. Sean lied compulsively, about anything and everything. He suffered from ADHD and impulsive outbursts of anger. He refused help in the morning, paying little attention to the staff's instructions on how to pack his backpack. Upon our departure, I noticed Sean's backpack leaning dramatically to the left. As we hiked through a lovely forest, Sean shared stories that revealed his hurt and anger toward his mother and stepfather. He also interrupted himself several times during the discussion to complain about his backpack. As we walked, I became confused several times by whether he was describing the pain of carrying the pack or the pain he felt in his family. Ultimately I realized it didn't matter; he was learning how to feel. In the process he was developing the kind of strength that only comes from experiencing the journey.

Most people attend parenting classes, buy books, or watch television shows with the expectation of acquiring new skills that will help them change the behavior of their children. This comes from a place of

walking therapy and connection with others ~Lyndsey

love. They don't want their children to experience pain or to struggle with painful symptoms. As parents, it is so easy to believe that it is our sole responsibility to make our children's lives as contented as we possibly can, to alleviate their every suffering, to soothe them as much as we are able, and to dedicate ourselves to comforting them and providing for them every opportunity available.

Our identity as parents may even lead us to think that if our children are struggling or suffering, we are "bad" mothers and fathers.

Facilitating the resolution of pain in our children is instinctual and perhaps even a function of our evolution as a species. It takes us working on our own buried feelings and issues for us to be able to provide a safe container for our children. When the things they do, express, or struggle with trigger us to try to control or avoid, then we are not really attending to their needs. Rather, we are operating from some old framework, some old context where we suffered ourselves. And if we operate from that context, it is almost impossible to see, connect, and attend to our children's needs. Dr. Daniel Siegel describes in his book how he found it difficult to stay present with his crying infant son. What he discovered was that the feeling stemmed from his time in a pediatric internship, when he had to work on very sick babies. He and his medical partner would have to take turns holding the screaming babies down while they administered treatment to them. To do so, Siegel had to block out the child's screams in order to provide lifesaving medical treatments.

The greatest gift, and sometimes the greatest challenge for us, is to stay connected to our children.

This connection is one of the most important contributions we can make to our children and their resiliency. Humans can endure a great deal when they know they are "okay." If at least one person "finds" them, they can often find themselves—and that is one of the most stabilizing forces in the human psyche. Since this task of connection may be difficult, and nebulous at times, we will talk about a set of tools that will provide specificity to this task.

Recently, I heard a father seek counsel from a few friends at a dinner gathering. He expressed frustration and angst about a problem he was experiencing with his two sons. His older son, Matthew, age eleven, was bullying his younger son, Todd, age six. What's worse, sometimes the bullying was quite violent. The father had tried punishing, lecturing, and threatening Matthew, but nothing seemed to work. He discerned that Matthew was expressing some buried jealousy or anger, and acknowledged that this acting out was an expression of those emotions.

He added, "What makes it even more difficult is the effect this behavior is having on my wife. She is at her wits' end with the bullying and I can't stand to see her so upset. She is a good mother and is doubting herself." Some friends suggested a harsher punishment; others suggested he take Matthew to a therapist. As the advice accumulated, the father said, "Maybe I will take him to therapy. He needs to be able to get to whatever is bothering him."

I asked, "What stops *you* from being the one he can talk to? You obviously see him. Why can't you listen to him?"

He responded, "I guess I just get too angry. For Todd and for my wife, the bullying has to stop. I get so angry that I am unable to sit and be patient enough to hear what he is feeling. If I could, maybe I could find a way for him to get his needs met in a healthy way." I didn't say anything, but it was right there in front of us. That is the thing that the child needs: getting the feelings out. That isn't what happens on the way to the solution; that *is* the solution.

If we can learn to tell our stories, and if we can be present enough to listen to others tell their own stories, then we have arrived at the solution. The solution is feeling it and talking about it. That is why communication skills are so central to the parent's curriculum, because

THE JOURNEY OF THE HEROIC PARENT

they provide the family with a healthy outlet for difficult and painful emotions. And if we are to create a space for our children to express themselves, we must first figure out what prevents us from seeing through the symptoms to the unexpressed emotions underneath. The next step is to equip ourselves with skills that support that process.

CHAPTER FOUR

FOUNDATIONS FOR CONNECTION

Communication skills help us connect to our children and our-selves. As we become more clear about the relationship between the events in our lives, our thoughts, and our feelings, we will be better able to see our children and provide them with a safe context in which to work through their difficulties.

THE ESSENCE OF THIS BOOK IS HOW TO *THINK* ABOUT PAR-enting, not the specific skills of parenting. If we focus too much on tools and techniques, we run the risk of ignoring the underlying principles. What is most important is understanding our own intent and how that reflects on our relationship with our children. Otherwise we may employ specific skills to gratify an agenda that is not based on the child's needs but rather our own. Skills are easy to absorb when we have clarity and awareness but almost impossible to understand when we are lost. Over the years I have seen many therapists focus on the tools and miss the principles altogether. Instituting a certain rule in communication without understanding the intent and the underlying principle reduces parents and students to puppets.

Thus, more important than the skills themselves are how we hold our children in our minds. Or to put it another way: what we think about the other person is more important than what we say to them. Once we regard the other with love and without judgment, our skills—particularly our communication skills—can provide clarity and connection. When we nest our communication skills in love, positive regard, and authenticity, our ability to communicate honestly and clearly will follow. A very simple way to understand the impact of how we hold the child in our mind is this:

> *How we think about our children is*
> *how they will think about themselves.*

Techniques don't address this. Techniques can be used to stretch us as parents but won't have a significant impact unless we change the way in which we regard our children.

At a conference I attended some time ago, someone suggested to the participating therapists, "If you do not like your client, please do not treat them. Please. And you can't fake it."

Why can't we fake it? The unconscious of the parent and the child are communicating with each other outside of either's awareness. And when we use skills without an understanding of our own internal process, we are likely to leak our unspoken agenda. This dissonance is a fundamental roadblock to connection because what we are saying is not what we are meaning. Skills do not connect people, but they can be the vehicles through which connection is made.

CHANGING OUR RELATIONSHIPS

When we use healthy communication skills built upon a foundation of deeper principles and understanding, we create a safe place for our children and beckon them out of self-medicating symptoms and into genuine feeling. Communication skills become the tools for unpacking the pain beneath the symptoms.

To be clear, communication is *not* a tool for changing the behavior of others. (Behavior change will be addressed in chapter five.) Again, the goal is not to change the other to make ourselves feel better. If we do that, we are implicitly telling our children that it is their job to make others happy, which predisposes them to lose themselves and can also create vulnerability to peer pressure. Rather, we use healthy communication skills as a way of allowing two people to be fully present in their relationship. When I teach parents not to use their feelings and their words to try to guilt their children into behavior change, I am often misinterpreted as saying, "Don't tell your child how you feel." Far from it. My point is:

> *We tell our children how we feel so we can*
> *be present with them and more intentional*
> *in our response to them.*

We tell our children how we feel as a way of sharing, not judging. But there may or may not be feedback implicit in the feelings we share. The feedback may or may not lead to action or change. We don't want our children to believe that when someone in their life has an emotional response to them and their actions—even when that person loves them—that they need to change or behave in a certain way for that person's satisfaction.

When I tell my children how I feel, another advantage is that I can clarify my own emotions and own them, rather than acting out on my children. If I can own it and then share it, I can get out of my own way and proceed toward a response that is healthier, grounded, and takes into account the child's needs. In essence, the message I send is something like this:

I am angry and frustrated at your behavior. You don't have to do anything about those feelings; those feelings are mine. It might help you to know how I am feeling. You can look at what you are doing, but I don't want you to change just because I am upset. I am going to take some time and sort out what I am feeling and then we are going to talk about what's going on with you. There may be a consequence, but if I decide what that is right now, I am afraid it is going to be based on my anger and not what you truly need.

INCREASING AWARENESS

In addition to the interpersonal benefits, communication skills provide a great tool for improving one's self-awareness. In my early days as a therapist, I was excited to try out the *I feel* approach on a relative. After I shared my heartfelt, carefully practiced statement, my aunt said, "Well, that's not true. How the hell did you come to that ridiculous conclusion?" At first I was crushed because I believed that if I was able to articulate my feelings correctly she would surely respond better than she had in the past. My wife said to me, "Wow, that didn't go well. I bet you'll think long and hard now before you encourage people to give *I feel* statements in a simplistic, solution-focused way." "I'll have to think about that," I told her. But I realized when I walked away from that very hurtful interaction that I was still glad I did it, glad I said my piece. Even though the person didn't reflect, didn't hear, and didn't validate, I experienced a sense of clarity and empowerment.

If the other person—whether it be your child or anyone in your life— is unavailable or unwilling to participate, then the *intrapersonal* goal is to understand how your perceptions and feelings are both distinct and connected. This differentiation is the task of being aware of oneself and capable of having both strong emotions and logical thoughts, as well as knowing the difference between the two and how they relate.

The most powerful source in us is accessed through our increasing self-knowledge. When we understand that events and beliefs are separate, then all of a sudden we start to understand ourselves at a deeper level. We gain more choices in how we deal with things. These tools provide light to give us a sense of where we came from, the context of where we grew up. Understanding our context allows us to separate ourselves from it. And when we separate from it, we can choose our life and our relationships instead of being a passive observer or victim stuck in the same patterns.

Many parents will challenge me on this concept of communication as a way of stating how you feel rather than leading toward a change or result. They'll say, "Well, I can't just reflect back to my child and then leave everything hanging." But if the goal is communication, then yes, you can do *just that*.

When you're reacting to something, you're often not really hearing the other person. Instead, you're treating them as if they are merely a mirror, and their assertion is about you. But the "I feel" statements you hear from your children and others aren't necessarily about you.

> *The capacity to listen is rooted in a strong sense of self.*

When you react in any way other than reflecting and hearing, you're not truly connecting to that person. You're being triggered by your own emotions and *making* the communication about you. Connecting is about having the clarity, confidence, peace, and strength to be able to *just hear* the other person.

THE NUTS AND BOLTS OF CONNECTING WITH OTHERS

It would be wonderful if a therapist could simply say, "Be intimate. Be close, but have clear boundaries. Don't be enmeshed. Be appropriately connected to each other" and it would magically happen. The truth is, people usually don't know how to do these things. Learning these communication skills can provide you with a roadmap toward communicating and connecting. As you utilize this map, you may encounter detours and setbacks, but even the bumps in the road will give valuable information about what is going on inside of you.

What follows is a step-by-step manual for the communications skills we use with families who participate in our program. While the information in this chapter is critical, the details may be more appealing after you have completed the entirety of this book. Over the years, many parents have reported to me that their understanding of these communication skills deepened over time and they were grateful for the detailed examples that were given to help them navigate their relationships when things got tricky.

The "I feel" statement is key. It's the way that intimacy looks in its simplest, most concrete form. Structurally speaking, "I feel" allows two people to connect but also to remain separate, and that's the ideal of differentiation, intimacy, and clarity. It's connection and separation at the same time.

"I Feel" Statement:

I feel _____ (emotion) _____ .

I feel this way when _____ (description of the event) _____ .

I feel this way because I think _(beliefs/interpretations/perceptions)_ .

What I hope that is within my control is _____ .

What I hope that I cannot control is _____ .

There are many different versions of this skill, but this is the one we utilized when we launched our program for adolescents. Start with "I feel" and then insert an emotion. It could be: happy, mad, sad, glad, or scared. One of the most common mistakes at this stage is to use language like "I feel *like* . . ." or "I feel *that* . . ." If you add "like" or "that," then you are discussing thoughts, not feelings. Statements like "I feel *like* it is time to leave" or "I feel *that* you are angry at me" do not express an emotion. The statement "I feel worried when you raise your voice because I think you are angry at me," on the other hand, expresses the sentiment but adds the appropriate emotional content.

The "I feel this way *when*" portion of the statement is important because it gives context to the feelings. A mother might say to her daughter, "I feel *this way* when you and I are talking about the hurt and anger you felt toward me when I restricted you from going to that party Saturday night."

It can be helpful to consider yourself as an outside observer of an event and describe it from a dispassionate third-person point of view. Otherwise, you may be tempted to try to influence and manipulate the listener by describing the "when" in an inflammatory manner. For example: "I feel sad. I feel this way when you are being a complete and total jerk." The trick is to present the event itself, not an interpretation or analysis of it. Rather than, "I feel scared when you get mad at me," try saying, "I feel scared when you raise your voice." The former is an interpretation of an event, while the latter focuses on the event itself.

Once you have presented the event dispassionately, you will have the opportunity to explain why you are feeling the way you are, and—combined with the interpretation of that event—what you believe precipitated your emotional reaction. This sets the stage for self-awareness and for understanding your wants, needs, and hopes.

> "I feel *this way* because I think that your ability to express your hurt and anger to me will increase our feelings of closeness, even if it is difficult in the moment."

Try not to use this step to sneak in a lecture to your child or to go on repeating and emphasizing the same ideas in different form. This is an abuse of the spirit of the "I feel" statement. I call this weaponizing the skill (and I admit that sometimes I am guilty of this in arguments with loved ones). If you do this, you are making the critical error of using the "I feel" statement to control behavior rather than to express yourself authentically and to connect emotionally.

You needn't worry about whether or not your words are insightful. What you're feeling may well be irrational, but it's still valuable. It can lead you to self-reflection and analysis, as well as to confronting some of your previously unchallenged beliefs.

The next step is when you make a distinction between what you can control (yourself) and what you can't control (others). This is your chance to focus awareness on your hopes, wants, and needs. These are what motivate us.

> "What I hope for myself is that I can continue to express my emotions clearly when I communicate with you, that I can let you have your feelings, and that I can support you in solving your problems."

I have always found it interesting that this step in the process is so difficult for parents. I think it is because we spend much of our energy trying to get others to change, and we don't consider the things over which we actually have power. For instance, if the issue is your son smoking pot and you are worried because you think it might harm him, where do you go when you examine what you can control? Our relationship with our children and their problems is so mixed up that we lose the ability to identify where we fit into the equation. Using this scenario, I would encourage a parent to consider saying something like,

> "What I hope for myself is that I can be consistent and strong and come to understand the most helpful way to respond to your drug use."

Again, having the awareness of what you have control over and what you don't will go a long way toward liberating you from guilt or engaging in power struggles.

The final step involves making a further distinction regarding control. This in an opportunity to express to others your hopes, desires, and needs in a context that does not manipulate them into behaving as you wish. This is your opportunity to tell your son or daughter (or to have them tell you) what decisions, actions, feelings, and future events you hope they would choose or experience. This is a demand-free wish list that you can express to your child in a neutral way, with no expectation that he comply with your wishes.

> "What I hope outside of my control is that you will feel comfortable enough to continue to share your hurt, anger, and challenges with me so that we can continue to make progress in our relationship."

The fact that the request for change in the other is stated in this way makes it much more likely that your child will actually consider your wants, needs, and desires—voluntarily.

When we began writing the curriculum for our adolescent wilderness program, we debated whether we should include this step at all. Some argued that if the communication skill was not intended to get the other person to change, then why give the sender a platform to make a request for change? My argument, however, was that just because the *want* for others to change was not spoken overtly and clearly, that didn't mean that it didn't exist. By putting the request out there, in a clear and open way, we carve out a space for genuine communication that is less likely to be perceived as manipulative. In families, and in every kind of relationship, hidden agendas are more corrosive than transparent ones.

Interestingly, the brightest parents that I deal with are, at times, incapable of distinguishing what they can and cannot control. To illustrate how we sometimes believe that our control extends beyond ourselves, ask yourself, "Who will ensure that I get a raise at work?" The first thought for most people is, "Me. I'm responsible for getting a raise." The actual answer is your boss. Your boss is in charge of deciding whether or not you get a raise. You are, of course, in charge of working hard, arriving to work on time, being creative, being energetic, giving good customer service, creating a good product—all of those things. But you are not in charge of the decision to give yourself a raise. Of course, if your boss is a good boss and he or she is paying attention, then he or she is going to give you a raise if it is deserved. However, it is possible for a horrible employee to receive many raises, and it's also possible for a great employee to receive none.

The kids in our wilderness program get very adept at recognizing control. And as they master it, they learn to let go of that which they cannot change. They learn that no one has to agree with them or give them what they want if they are upset. They learn about the delay of gratification and the tolerance of frustration. They learn that happiness comes from inside. They learn that the only real freedom, the freedom that matters, comes from focusing on what is in their control. These changes can prepare them to reengage with their parents without the powerful urge to guilt, manipulate, or bully. And just as important, as parents see their children making this progress, first with the therapists, and then with them, they begin to understand that they don't have to "*make* their children happy" by compromising, avoiding honesty, or compromising their own values.

By the sixth or seventh day of the program, the children can hear things that parents don't hear. They'll recognize when a parent is mixing up an event with a belief about an event or an interpretation of an event. They'll detect a parent's confusion about what they can and can't control. Developing this new awareness is powerful for them. It is often in those moments when we realize we can't change others that we return our focus onto ourselves; as Frankl points out, "When we are no longer able to change a situation, we are challenged to change ourselves."

REFLECTIVE LISTENING

After the sender shares their "I feel" statement, the receiver's job is simply to paraphrase it back to them. Some call this active listening or deep listening. Basically, you respond, "So what you're saying is . . ." and then repeat it—but in your own words. You don't interpret, react, negate, or minimize anything; you simply reiterate it without judgment. Remember, even if the other person doesn't give a perfect "I feel" statement, you can still practice reflecting. In fact, learning to hear all the parts of an "I feel" statement, even the unspoken ones, can be very helpful in avoiding escalations or conflict.

Reflective Listening:

You feel _____ (emotion) _____ .

You feel this way when _____ (event description) _____ .

You feel this way because you think _____
_____ (beliefs/interpretations/perceptions) .

What you hope for yourself is _(something inside their control)_ .

What you hope for others is _(something outside their control)_ .

After completing this reflective listening exercise, it's important to check if you got it right, or if anything was missed. Continue to reflect until the other party agrees that you heard them accurately. It's okay to ask questions. "Can you help me with what you said? I forgot what you are feeling or I forgot what you were thinking." There's no failure if you ask for help. In fact, asking questions implies that you are engaged in the process and want to hear what the other person is saying. We often lose contact with the other person because something is triggered in us and we are too busy thinking about our rebuttal, about what we can say to get them to think or feel differently. If you're doing that, you are neither connecting nor listening. If you are truly engaged and asking appropriate, respectful questions, you are on the right path.

By asking "Did I get it right, or was there anything else?" you are neither endorsing their truth or agreeing with everything the other party says. It is simply a reiteration of understanding. If somebody says to you, "I believe the moon is made out of cheese," you reflect back and say, "So you believe the moon is made out of cheese. Did I hear you correctly?"

Just the other day, my youngest daughter asked me if she could play with our large dogs on the couch. I told her, "No, but you can play with them here or there." Frustrated and sad, she responded, "That is not fair." I said, offering her empathy, "I know... right?" She then raised her brows and exclaimed, "So I can?" "No," I said, "I agree with you that it is unfair, but the answer is still no." This kind of simple exchange serves to illustrate how people can easily confuse being heard with agreement.

The good news is that over time our children and others can learn that it is okay to feel or think something that we do not endorse but that we do hear and understand. That, almost by definition, is the demonstration of intimacy: the contact of two separate selves.

My all-time favorite professor in college was also one of the greatest therapists I have ever met. There were six of us in her doctoral class, and she was late all the time—it was one of her few character flaws. I was elected by the other class members to give an "I feel" statement to her when she arrived. When she walked into the room I said, "Leslie, I am feeling very frustrated that you are late again."

She responded by simply, compassionately, and empathically responding, "I bet you are!" And then she was quiet.

I then realized, "Oh, that's my feeling." I could have reported her to the dean. I could have dropped her class, and she would have let me. I could have tried to guilt and manipulate her. But that moment of her listening and hearing what I had to say and having the strength of ego to just let me feel what was true for me led me to own my feelings. When we as receivers give explanations and justifications, we are not successfully identifying a lack of understanding or insight on the part of the sender. Instead, we are exposing our own anxiety.

BEYOND COMMUNICATION 101

Over the years as I have engaged families in communication-skills training, I have observed some subtle ways in which they get stuck as they try to implement the "I feel" statement. The following are some principles or sub-skills that might help you steer clear of those pitfalls.

Discovering hidden agendas in our communication. The goal of these communication skills is to uncover what we are "really" saying. A large part of a therapist's training is learning to perceive the *process* of communication over the *content* of communication—and in our own relationships that is difficult at times. *Meta-message* refers to the meaning of the communication or the message beneath the message. We all know what it feels like when our parent or spouse says one thing to us and means something else. This meaning could be intended or subconscious on the part of the person saying it. Honesty, self-awareness, and transparent dialogue are the simplest ways to improve the consistency between what is said and what is meant. Meta-messages come from the context, from roles in the relationship between sender and receiver, and include nonverbal cues and covert agendas.

We can often discover the meta-message by asking ourselves tough questions about our intent. Practicing the "I feel" statement may uncover our authentic motivations. Healthy communication is about bringing together our words and our intended message.

Avoiding language traps. One of the simplest and most effective par-enting tools I have found is eliminating the use of imperatives. It sounds easier than it actually is. Avoid command words and phrases such as "you should," "you have to," "you must," "you need to"' "you've got to" and judgmental words such as "good," "bad," "right," and "wrong." I once heard someone refer to these as "red-light" phrases because they tend to build barriers to communication. Imperatives invite defensiveness, and often stem from insecurity rather than confidence. They provide the sender with a feeling of security from a false sense of control. People assume that imperatives are powerful because they refer to an objective truth, but in fact the opposite is true. What one feels is what one feels—that cannot be argued with. Right and wrong, on the other hand, can be debated ad nauseam.

Another example of how changing our words can help us discover a new way of thinking is to avoid black-and-white or all-or-nothing state-ments. I heard one student start to say, "Well, it always—" I jumped in: "What were you about to say?" And he replied, "Well, I was about to say 'It always happens this way.'" And I said, "What are you changing it to?" He, in turn, replied, "Well, it seems like this happens to me a lot." And just that little change in wording created a shift in tone and ultimately led to empowerment.

When I invite parents and students to stop using imperatives, to use "I" statements, and to avoid extreme all-or-nothing statements, I see them become much more thoughtful, intentional, and deliberate. This clarity leads to intimacy in their relationships. By changing the words we use, we can begin to affect how we think.

Stating your intent, or preparing the listener. An important facet to this communication model is stating your intent. You'll be amazed by how much better people will listen to you when you set it up by saying, "I just want to give you an 'I feel' statement, and I just want to be heard." By stating our goals for others at the onset of a discussion, we can be clearer. We are more likely to match what we are saying with what we are meaning. This also helps you get out of the rut of trying to change someone's opinion. If you're using an "I feel" statement to punish, control, guilt, or change someone, stating your intent beforehand will tease that out. You'll either realize it and take a step back and consider your intent, or you'll own it ("I want you to be convinced"). This transparency frees up others from an obligation to respond in the way that you want them to respond.

Remember, the goal is not behavior change. We use feelings to try to get others to change. We often do this because it is how we were raised. We were taught that if Mom or Dad got upset then it was our job to change our behavior to rectify it. If somebody gives me an "I feel" statement and I reflect it back, then I've heard him or her. Just listening to someone is not actively doing anything, not fixing anything, and not attempting to change a behavior. But it is *containing* the other person.

When I am able to hear you, I am providing a safe place for you to be who you are, where you are allowed to *feel*, wholly and completely. There isn't a "look on the bright side" speech that follows. For instance, if your child comes home and says, "My teacher doesn't like me," you wouldn't say, "Well, you just have to try harder." You won't fall into the trap of making dismissive comments like that if you're strictly reflecting. This is a hard thing to do, especially as a parent, because most of us are fixers. Most of us are uncomfortable with other people's uncomfortable feelings, so our response often sends the message of "don't feel." Over the years, many clients have shared that, while growing up, they were not allowed to feel certain things in their family. Now I doubt that very many people have a list on the refrigerator door that lays out rules like "don't feel sad" or "don't feel angry." Yet the kinds of interactions we often engage in with others communicate just that type of message.

A few years ago, my youngest child was riding in the car with two friends, and one of the children started to cry about not getting her way. "You're going to have to cry more quietly," said the friend's mother, "you know, it's not that bad."

"My mom is nicer than you because she lets me be sad when I am sad," my daughter interjected. Even my five-year-old daughter could see the kindness in allowing a child to express her feelings—even if those feelings were unpleasant.

When you employ this skill of reflection, you can help avoid rescuing, dismissing, or discounting the feelings of others.

Dueling "I feel" statements. Often a sender's "I feel" statement elicits emotions in the listener. The risk here is that if the listener responds with their own "I feel" statement, this might feel dismissive to the sender.

The desire to return an "I feel" statement with one's own should always be delayed. Please try to remember that this construct is designed for a reason; you are providing your child a different experience.

Dialogue, as opposed to listening, may be counterproductive. Give others the space to feel and express their feelings. The delay between statements could be five minutes or five days, but it is crucial that the sender feels free of competition. If necessary, the listener can always say, "Now I have an 'I feel' statement I would like to share. Are you open to it now, or would you like me to just listen and share it later?"

Clarifying facts. Another common pitfall I encounter when people use this skill is an immediate desire to clarify facts. "What if the facts of my child's 'I feel' statement aren't true?" they might ask. "What if the thought, belief, or event didn't really happen? I'm sure you're going to make some room for me to clarify that." My answer is always simple: "No," I say. "I'm not."

This is one of the most challenging aspects of communication because it is so easy to discount the original statement and thereby invalidate the sender's feelings. Remember, it is the sender's *subjective reality* that matters—therefore, there is no objective truth that needs clarification.

Again, after reflecting upon one's "I feel" statement, you may inform the sender that you have a reaction, whether it be a clarification of facts or a different opinion, and ask if it is okay to assert it or if she'd prefer you wait until another time. This way the sender decides whether or not she is open to a discussion about facts, intent, or interpretation. And implicitly the receiver has made it known, just by virtue of the question, that he is not in agreement—but without arguing.

Again, the objective truth concerning an event is not what's important. People often exaggerate or stretch truth to get the validation they crave. You can imagine yourself doing this. Something happens at work, or a friend does something to you, and in telling the story to your spouse you find yourself magnifying certain details. In doing so, you're saying to yourself, "I have a right to feel hurt and angry—even if I have to make the story a little bit more fantastic. I have a right to feel this way." That's one facet of exaggeration. We do it because we're afraid that if we tell the story as it really happened, it won't be good enough or illustrate our point clearly enough.

If your child exaggerates when telling a story related to his feelings, let him. You'd be surprised how often children eventually tone down their initial stories once they feel as if they've been heard and their feelings validated.

Embellishment is a natural human response. Many of us learned to exaggerate as children precisely because our parents or caregivers suggested that we didn't have the right to our emotions.

A few years ago I was working with Seth, a young man from a divorced family. While his parents acted pleasant enough toward each other, they both harbored resentments from years of turbulent marriage. Seth's mother said her ex-husband had been verbally abusive toward her and the children. Seth's father said his ex-wife emotionally recruited and indoctrinated their children in collusion against him. Seth saw his father much like his mother did, abusive and even went further to assert that his dad was physically violent. He was committed to his story and did not waver from it, even though he knew his father would deny it. As a result of these dynamics, and after some unsuccessful attempts at family therapy over the years, Seth's father developed an acute distrust of therapists and therapy in general. He was not an easy client to work with, and sometimes his disdain for the process leaked into his letters to Seth. Ultimately, Seth admitted to both his father and me that he was angry and resentful at his dad's outbursts, some of which involved slapping or hitting. His father vehemently denied any such behavior. Although Seth's mother had a lot of negative views about her ex-husband, she echoed that her son's accusations of physical abuse were patently false.

A saying we use in therapy is that the truths of facts (except in the case of reportable abuse) are not important; if someone feels something, then it is true for them. I encouraged Seth's dad to listen to his son without correcting him, to demonstrate his willingness to give the young man a chance to recount his history as he remembered it. It took some extra calls on my part to convince Seth's father to just *listen to* his son, and his skepticism of therapists grew stronger than ever. "Trust me," I said to him. "Your son will come closer to you and to a shared version of things if you just listen to him."

In the following weeks, Seth ended up admitting to his father during a visit, "I was really scared when you would yell at me, but you never hit me. You never hit mom. You never hit my brother. I exaggerated the facts because they were my way of talking about how small and how powerless I felt in the face of your anger."

Then, on the day of Seth's graduation from our program, his father began to cry. It was a very significant event because he had almost never cried as an adult—and certainly never in front of anyone else. Through tears, he thanked his son for acknowledging the exaggerations. He then told me that although he had held very little faith in my initial advice to simply listen, the breakthrough with his son had taught him a powerful lesson. During their final family session, we all shed tears, hugged, and said our good-byes. I left that day with a reminder of the healing power of truly listening and empathizing.

"Give me an example." While seemingly benign, the listener's request for an example can be problematic. An example is just that: an example. The example is not the feeling. What's important in this exercise is the feeling, and the sender's ownership of that feeling. Furthermore, asking for an example is often just a roundabout way of debating the facts, and sends the message that the sender needs to justify or prove her feelings. In essence, what you are saying in doing so is, "Give me another example of a situation that led to this feeling and we will discuss if you have the facts right or if your feeling is valid."

There is certainly a place in healthy communication for specific examples. The problem is that too often our examples are exaggerated and inflammatory. We use examples from unresolved issues or use examples as a passive way to pile on. Similar to recruiting, "Other people think the same thing about you," we use examples as proof for the validity of the emotion.

So, if you are going to employ examples in your communication, do it slowly and intentionally. Prefacing your response with something like "I am going to give an example that is different but may have some features that will help you understand where I am coming from" may help reduce debate. If you're on the listening end, suspend your literal assessment of the example and try to hear the emotional thread that ties the current situation and the example together. Doing so will make you a better listener, one less likely to be defensive or argumentative.

Invite a reaction from others, and be open to the response. After giving an "I feel" statement, you have to decide too whether you are ready for a response after your listener's reflection. If you are, you have to be open. This is a very precarious skill and people often struggle with it. Parents often ask, "Do you want me to respond to that?" When the child says yes, I first interject, "Whoa, are you sure? Because I'm pretty sure your mom and dad feel differently. Are you ready to hear that? Or is that the first step into an old argument?" If you ask for a reaction, you must be open to the response. If you find yourself getting off track, it's okay to say, "You know what? I wasn't ready for your response. This part of the conversation needs to be about me stating my feelings and being heard."

Ask questions that are questions and make statements that are statements. You may have heard the phrase "say what you mean and mean what you say." To this I add "a question is a question and a statement is a statement." Oftentimes I hear people disguising their questions as statements. For instance: "Don't you think that it would be great if you did this?" What that really means is, "I think it'd be great if you did this." This is a kind of "leading the witness" question that many people feel trapped by. If you have a question, ask it. If you have a statement, state it. This is simple but by no means automatic. It may take practice and coaching. In my experience, it often takes a third party to help tell the difference.

"Why" doesn't always mean "why?" One of the oldest traps in communication is the "Why?" question. Whether or not it's intentional, the word "why" is often an invitation to argue. For example, "Why did you do that?" often really means "I am upset and don't like what you did." Or when a child asks, "Why does it have to be this way?" she may really be trying to say, "I don't like it and want to debate your thinking on this matter."

In these situations, the receiver can help by trying one of three things: First, reflect the underlying emotion. "When you ask 'Why?' what I hear is that it's upsetting or frustrating for you." Second, ask the sender if they really need information, or if the why is meant as a substitute for a feeling. Third, answer the question and see where it goes. If the sender really is just looking for clarification on the why, then the answer will resolve the issue quickly.

Empathy. Empathy goes beyond the skill of reflecting and involves connecting with what the other person is feeling. Here are a couple examples that illustrate empathy:

Daughter: "I felt hurt when my friends rejected me for turning down drugs."

Mother: "I understand what it feels like to have people you care about turn away from you."

Wife: "I am so frustrated at work, and my boss does not seem to listen to anything I suggest."

Husband: "I'm sorry, I hate it when I am not heard."

These kinds of responses can go a long way, but you don't want to overdo it and risk appearing as if you're trying to one-up the other person with your own story. Many times a simple "Oh, that's tough" or "Yeah, I hate that too" will suffice. Again, the language here isn't important. These examples simply illustrate the ideal ways of thinking about the other.

Searching for primary vs. secondary emotions. Secondary emotions are emotions we use to cover up a more vulnerable, sensitive, or "primary" emotion. Secondary emotions can be considered defensive emotions, and are usually emotions close to anger. We might feel sad, hurt, embarrassed, or powerless, but instead of owning these more vulnerable emotions, we instead express anger, frustration, or rage. These secondary emotions often distance us from others. If I am hurt, it is easier to be angry because anger puts a wall between you and me and prevents me from getting hurt by you again. Angry emotions also tend to point fingers at others' behaviors and minimize ownership, which feels vulnerable.

Be careful to ask someone to access and express a primary emotion; it may be too soon, and too threatening, for the sender to share his vulnerability. The receiver is best advised to listen and accept the secondary emotion in the "I feel" statement. With trust and experience as a foundation, the sender can more easily access a more raw emotion.

Sharing primary emotions with your children is a great way to model vulnerability and create safety in a parent-child relationship.

Anger is often the door we walk through to find the other, so it is okay to take what is given.

Why we struggle with assertive communication. It's much easier to blame someone else for your problems than to acknowledge your own feelings. It is much easier to say, "You're a jerk" than to say, "I felt hurt." The latter gives away power, and the former preserves it. But you have to own your feelings if you're going to be vulnerable and allow yourself to open up and connect. Owning one's feelings is *the* prerequisite for intimacy between parent and child, husband and wife—all relationships.

As humans, we often put the blame on others. It is much easier to fight than it is to set boundaries or show vulnerability. It is much easier to prepare a defense—to control, lecture, correct, or teach—than to truly listen to and connect with the other. Sometimes I joke that what allows me to hear my wife is pretending that she is talking about *some other idiot husband* so that I can avoid taking offense and instead just listen to what she has to say.

Healthy communication skills are often going to be met with resistance, at least initially. That's okay. Stick with it. Many complain, "This isn't natural. This feels contrived." It's okay—and maybe even helpful—to try something new. Indeed, new skills usually feel awkward. The intent in this construct is to disrupt old patterns that may be comfortable but are also problematic. Discomfort is just one more part of the hero's journey. When introducing these communication skills, I always encourage people to practice continually. Over time, if you diligently hone these skills, you'll be amazed how all of your relationships change for the better, starting with the relationship with yourself.

It's simple—almost too simple. It may seem beneath you, but it's where the hard work is accomplished. I heard the following story years ago about the great cellist Pablo Casals. He died in 1973 at the age of ninety-six, and on the day he died he was practicing the scales. It's a reminder that even the best among us at a certain task or a skill need the fundamentals. We have to remember to keep it simple.

CONCLUSION

As parents, we can learn to listen so that we may connect. We can learn to listen without judgment, without fears, without control. We can practice the skill of truly hearing our children. We can clear our mind of rebuttals, of arguments, of corrections, of retorts.

Some time ago, I was driving with my three-year-old daughter. As we approached a stoplight, she said, "Red means go. Green means stop." I gently taught her the correct association of the stoplights and wondered how all those hours of watching *Dora the Explorer* had failed us. A few days later, the interaction repeated itself. Finally, looking back in the rearview mirror, I saw her looking out the window to her right, at the stoplight on the street intersecting ours. "Green means stop, Daddy." She was right. The light, from her view, showed green when we stopped, and red when we accelerated. I just needed to take a moment to see through her eyes.

A therapist described a client she had seen years ago. This client grew up near a river in rural Germany. During the course of her analysis, she would move back and forth between her early childhood and the present day. One afternoon, while the client was telling a story, it was unclear if the story was from the past or the present. The therapist didn't ask but somehow just knew: "I knew she was talking about the distant past because I could smell the river near her childhood home." Deep listening means that we gently hold the child in our minds and allow for all of him to be present.

In the movie *Bowling for Columbine*, Michael Moore explores the heartbreaking story of the Columbine tragedy. Apparently the shooters were fans of Marilyn Manson, the infamous shock rocker. Manson was blamed, among others, for his negative influence as a role model and his lyrics. In an interview, Moore asked Manson what he might have said to these two young men if he could have talked to them before that fateful morning. Manson replied, "I wouldn't have said anything. I would have listened."

A pivotal moment in my life occurred while I was struggling during my teen years. My therapist sat my mother and me in a room and made her sit there and just listen to me. She was not allowed to defend, pass judgment, clarify, or rebut. That experience told me, "You are not crazy. The anger, hurt, and fear you feel is real." Of course, the way I was acting out was dangerous, but feeling as if I could be heard gave me a safe place and an outlet for those feelings.

By listening, connecting, understanding, hearing, and validating, our children are better able to find themselves, and from this place they can come to believe they are okay.

And this *being okay* allows children to compassionately address issues that might be preventing healthy living.

During my own son's time in wilderness therapy, my wife and I were asked to come for a day visit. The goal was nebulous, but I assumed it was simply to connect, and possibly to provide his therapist with some background information for future family therapy work. When our youngest daughter, Isabella, only five at the time, asked where her brother had gone, the simple phrase we shared was that "he was in the mountains, learning how to be happy."

We made our trip out to the field area—getting lost only twice—and arrived in the evening at the boys' group. Our reunion was tender and tearful. It had been eight weeks since we had last seen Jake, and after hugs and greetings we sat down to learn about how and what he was doing. Although I had worked with hundreds of families as a wilderness therapist, I had never quite experienced the kind of joy I felt from seeing new growth and insight in my son.

The next day, the staff led Jake and me in an experiential activity. Jake had initially struggled to learn how to make a fire using the bow-drill, but had recently mastered the technique and was excited about his accomplishment. In the exercise, Jake was to blindfold me and instruct me how to make a fire. However, being a wilderness therapist, I had already grasped this particular skill years ago during my wilderness therapy training. I was so competitive that I would play games with my students and staff to see who could make a fire first. So when Jake blindfolded me and began to explain the technique, I regrettably grew impatient and just started grabbing the tools and getting to work. Soon Jake became silent as I forged ahead and began spinning my bow.

In the family therapy session that followed, when Jake's therapist asked why it was so hard for him to open up and talk with me, tears began to form in his eyes. "Because he is better at it," he replied. "Talking with my dad is like playing one-on-one with Kobe Bryant. He will always win. He will always be right." My heart broke at hearing this from my son. Even now, as I write this, my eyes well up with tears at the thought of how little space I left for my son to share his own thoughts and feelings. "It's like the bow-drill exercise you guys did together earlier," his therapist observed. "Your dad goes ahead without you, and eventually you just get silent."

We would be wise to give them more space to express themselves and be heard. One therapist told me years ago that the image of the perfect parent is one with his mouth taped shut. The developing child's brain as he comes into adulthood is full of new ideas and feelings, and that child becomes intimidated when attempting to engage with a parent whom they perceive has all the answers. You may believe yourself ready to provide your children with answers, wisdom, and stories that demonstrate your storehouse of all of the answers in life. This teacher-student dynamic is neither rewarding nor encouraging for a child who is just beginning to understand life and is struggling to articulate it.

The first thing we can do to encourage our children to talk more and to open up to us is shut our own mouths.

Asking questions of our children is not enough. We need to learn how to empty our minds and give space to them. Judgments, rebuttals, pep talks, and corrections from us give them the impression that they need to just shut up and listen to us. But through the art of listening, we create a *culture*—in our families and in our relationships—where listening without judgment is the norm. In time our loved ones begin to understand that we are just listening and neither agreeing nor disagreeing.

Part of giving space to your children also involves giving them permission to talk less, to talk slowly and not be rushed—to make small strides in their communication without being barraged by pointed questions. Our patience demonstrates that we are neither judging them nor making their situations about us. Asking a teenager to sit down for a talk often triggers glazed eyes and staring off into the distance while they wait for us to stop the lecture so they can move on to something else, something more enjoyable . . . pulling weeds, anything!

Sometimes making a point or sharing a feeling can be expressed without requiring anything at all from our children. It can be a series of very short conversations, each about five minutes long, where you talk about your thoughts, beliefs, and feelings. Don't necessarily ask for or expect them to respond, and be willing to end the discussion without the satisfaction of closure or consensus. Keep it short and keep it casual. Talk to your children while doing something else. I like to call this the "grocery store lecture."

Dinner, chores, and shopping are all great opportunities for a seemingly off-the-cuff conversation.

In these settings, the child's focus will be on something other than the parent. If they are involved in a task such as doing the dishes or making a fire at a campsite, their conscious minds are less likely to have free resources to react against perceived threats or intrusions.

Something else I suggest is to be the first one to stop a discussion or conversation. We are usually prone to talk or lecture, often repeating ourselves until we feel some sort of satisfaction or hear what we want to hear from our children. It can be more effective to have a very short talk—one to two minutes—and then be the first one to walk out of the room or change the subject. Initially, this method of communication will feel unsettling and unfinished, but this will help to teach our children that every discussion doesn't last forever.

Our children's sparse communication can stem from a need to protect themselves from a sense of being smothered or swallowed up. Be patient. Accept bits and pieces as good enough. This communicates to them that you are a receptive listener and that you are not ready to pounce on your child when they fall short of providing everything you want to hear. Developing this patience may take days, weeks, or even years, but we are in this with them for the long haul. Our eagerness for resolution is intimidating to our children because it feels like pressure on them.

In the end, the only thing we as parents can do is give our children more room to talk and to invite communication by showcasing healthy listening skills. Our impulse to force our children to communicate will likely lead to a more rigid, fearful, and terse response—the exact opposite of what we want.

Part of that message is that they need some distance from you. This is developmentally appropriate. Our angst and anxiety about that distance feels smothering, needy, and shaming to them.

> *Hear what they are not saying. Hear what their behavior tells you.*

Because we are involved with our children for the rest of our lives, we would do well to be patient, refrain from judgment, and wait for them to come to us. Stay with them as long as you can—and what I mean by that is that you learn to take care of yourself so they don't have to take care of you. Do your own work and learn to listen to and see them instead of letting them be eclipsed by your own childhood wounds.

CHAPTER FIVE

TOOLS FOR ENCOURAGING CHANGE IN OUR CHILDREN

Using behavioral tools is fine, but only if they are nested in love and awareness. And we would be wise to first listen to what the behavior is telling us before we launch into changing it.

THE MOST COMMON QUESTION I'M ASKED BY PARENTS IS how they can change their children's behavior. My answer is that the most effective way to facilitate a behavioral change in a child is to try *not to control* that behavior. It is easy for any parent-child relationship, especially during the child's adolescence, to devolve into a power struggle. We respond to the child's behavior out of fear, frustration, and anger, and it becomes less about helping her grow and more about our own catharsis. Still, parents want to know: What is an appropriate behavioral consequence? Will my child internalize it? Will it help or hurt our overall relationship?

It is a mistake to believe that providing consequences for your children means that you are not nurturing them. Emotional connection and disciplinary structure are best understood when we place them on two separate continuums. You can have a strict or permissive approach and be anywhere on the continuum. Likewise, you can also have a connected or distant approach.

Some parents may try to buy their children's affection and connection. This is particularly dangerous if it comes from the role reversal of asking our children to take care of our needs. Alice Miller warns us to avoid asking our children to give us what our parents did not. It is not our children's job to provide us unconditional love and acceptance. Parents complain that their teen doesn't show them the love and affection that they did in previous years, "They have moved away from me and seem to

One of the traps parents fall into is trying to repair the disconnected relationship they have with their children by becoming more permissive.

hate me." Providing us with a sense of security in the context of unconditional love was our parents' job. And it was difficult for them and they fell short. But we cannot solve that problem by asking our children to do it for us.

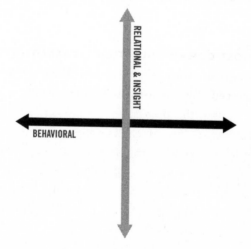

Many of us may have known an authority figure in our lives who started out strict and then eased up over time. There's a story from the book *The One Minute Manager* that describes two Chinese emperors.

The first emperor started off very strict and then loosened up during the course of his reign. The second emperor started off very permissive and eventually became more stringent. The subjects of the empire regarded the first emperor very highly and he was greatly loved; the second emperor was thought of as a tyrant and was not liked by his people. This story shows that beginning with strictness does not necessarily prevent a good relationship from developing between two people. In fact, sometimes it is the best foundation for the relationship.

Although the idea of control is discussed in a later chapter, it's important to underscore a few comments about it here. "Strict" does not mean "controlling," and "permissive" does not mean "relational." The matrix is more complex. Controlling parents use lectures, guilt, threats, debate, and domination to try to get their child to behave in certain ways. Permissive parents often attempt to negotiate, but these negotiations can lead to inconsistencies depending on the child's response, creating confusion and power struggles.

Many of the children who have attended our programs describe the experience with us as being one of the most freeing and liberating of their lives, despite the fact that the wilderness milieu is usually more strict than anything they've ever experienced. What this shows us is that strictness in itself is not the problem. Rather, it is how the structure is applied.

The wilderness setting also offers fewer privileges than most of the children are used to as well. Importantly, they know they are emotionally safe. They are allowed to like or hate the staff. Many of the rules, structures, and consequences are defined and nonnegotiable, but the students are allowed to disagree philosophically.

When children complain about being controlled, they are talking about emotional control.

It's like walking into a spider web: you can't always see it, but you can feel it. As parents, our goal is to create a small version of the world and show our children, "This is the way things work. This is the way respect works. This is the way kindness works. This is the way effort works. This is the way we do things in this family. We're going to have these rewards and privileges." I often tell my young clients in the wilderness, "I am not playing the role of God here. I'm playing the role of Isaac Newton. I didn't invent gravity, I'm just showing you how it works." That's also how I see the job of the parent using behavioral principles.

THE BASICS OF BEHAVIORAL REINFORCEMENT

Below is an image representing the four-box model of behavioral reinforcement. It demonstrates positive reinforcement, negative reinforcement, negative punishment, and positive punishment. It is important to understand this model, partly because the word "punishment" has such negative connotations.

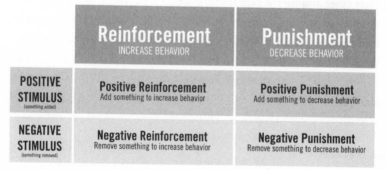

Operant Conditioning

	Reinforcement INCREASE BEHAVIOR	Punishment DECREASE BEHAVIOR
POSITIVE STIMULUS (something added)	**Positive Reinforcement** Add something to increase behavior	**Positive Punishment** Add something to decrease behavior
NEGATIVE STIMULUS (something removed)	**Negative Reinforcement** Remove something to increase behavior	**Negative Punishment** Remove something to decrease behavior

Since these terms are fairly academic, let's take a moment to explain each of the four approaches.

Positive reinforcement seems obvious at face value. You reward behavior that you want to see increase or continue. But one distinction worth making is the difference between positive reinforcement and bribery. With positive reinforcement, the reward comes *after* the behavior. With bribery, the reward comes *before* the behavior, thus by definition it does not reinforce. The risk with bribery is that motivation may wane over time. This approach also does not teach children to deal with a delay of gratification, a critical developmental task for them.

Negative reinforcement removes something to encourage an increase in a desired behavior. Your son does the dishes in order to avoid the nagging that often follows his leaving them until later, for instance.

Negative punishment removes something with the aim that undesired behavior will diminish. You take away a toy or privilege so that the child will stop fighting with siblings.

Positive punishment (what we commonly think of as punishment) provides an aversive consequence in an aim to decrease undesired behavior. A fine or speeding ticket are simple examples, as is having the child do some extra chores after she left a mess the previous day. A weakness of this kind of punishment is that it can often be a byproduct of anger. In such cases, it's not the child's needs that are being addressed but rather the parent's cathartic needs. Every parent is guilty of this from time to time, and this is especially true of parents of struggling children. To employ positive punishment effectively, ask yourself questions that highlight your intentions and execution. Another weakness is that punishment doesn't tell the child what *to* do.

Let your child "hate" you or "hate" the situation. Let him disagree with your reasoning and respond to it with whatever emotion he has. This illustrates the idea of letting go while simultaneously being firm and clear.

Many parents feel held hostage when their child accuses them of punishing. The parent may be responding with some residual anger held toward his or her own parents. This residual emotion could be the result of having felt humiliated, misunderstood, or punished for things in childhood that needed an outlet or expression. The pendulum need not swing all the way to the permissive and passive parenting style; instead, clarity and intentionality can be added to the equation to ensure the healthy use of positive and negative punishment.

UNDERSTANDING YOUR CHILD'S BEHAVIORS

Early behavioral theory focused solely on creating behavior change by any means necessary. *Functional analysis* is a behavioral term that means something is more complex than simple punishment and reward. A similar concept is the *function of the symptom*. It examines the context, meaning, and deeper purpose of behaviors. As a parent, that means you must look at what your child wants from life, what they hope to achieve, and combine that with an understanding of their previous and current behaviors. Your children do what they do because it works for them and because it's better than not doing it right now.

What does a child get out of a particular situation? What does he avoid by engaging in the behavior? The answer is different for everybody. Sometimes it's pain, sometimes it's discomfort, and sometimes it's work. A parent may come to me and say, "My son's living in my basement. He's twenty-three years old, he's smoking pot, and he doesn't have a job."

My response may be, "Not bad. He's got a good gig. I think that a lot of us might be tempted by that set up." That's part of functional analysis. It is critical to ask ourselves about our child's behavior and try to understand the benefits of the behavior before trying to change it.

Parents are often exasperated by their child's poor choices. The child is behaving in a way that goes against the family's values and morals. "Why does my child do this?" the parents often ask in desperation. Again, let me offer the simplest answer: *because it works*. Let's start with that conclusion and work our way backward to find out *how* it works and what results from the destructive decisions of the child.

In the 1960s, a team of sociologists, anthropologists, and psychologists founded the Mental Research Institute (MRI) in Palo Alto, California. This team was interested in systems, specifically family systems, and they wanted to understand the complex interactions and transactions that occurred within individual family units. They observed a number of families in their homes, where they witnessed a myriad of stressors: illness, job difficulties, learning difficulties, and more. Yet over the course of their research, they began to see that it was not the stressors that defined the family's problems, but rather the *solutions* that each family instituted to deal with them: Dad getting angry and yelling at a child for struggling in school, Mom nagging the children to clean up after themselves, a child hitting his brother for entering his room, or a child yelling at her sister for borrowing her dress. Thus, we see that it is not our actual problem that is truly the challenge; it is our attempt to solve that problem that becomes truly problematic.

Let's return to Jung's idea that neurosis is a substitute form of legitimate suffering. This statement mirrors the conclusions of the MRI group. Our children's symptoms, their behaviors that frustrate us so much, are merely their best attempts to alleviate their angry or hurt feelings and change their situations. Even though some of the choices our children make seem irrational, there is a simple logic at the root of their behavior:

> *The pain of this behavior is better than the pain that would come from not behaving in this way.*
>
> *I would rather be in trouble with my parents than continue to feel like an outsider among my peers.*
>
> *I would rather fail than feel the fear of failure.*
>
> *I would rather cut myself and feel that pain than have an absence of feeling.*
>
> *I would rather drink or smoke pot and feel this high rather than feel stressed or bored or insecure.*

I would rather piss off my parents than feel the crushing guilt and disappointment of trying to please them and failing.

This last sentiment surprises parents. I have worked with many students over the years who entered the program sporting the rough exterior of "I don't give a shit what you think about me," but ultimately revealed themselves to be haunted by the chronic anxiety of wanting to please others.

While lecturing at an eating disorder clinic, a staff member brought an example of this dynamic to my attention. A young anorexic woman showed up to one of my lectures on addiction and was confronted by the staff for wearing layers of oversized clothes. I later asked, "Doesn't layering and baggy clothing make them look heavier?"

She informed me, "Sometimes, they wear extra or baggy clothes because their low body weight leaves them susceptible to cold, or because they are trying to hide their low body weight from staff or from parents. Another reason, however, is that if they believe that others see them as fat, then they can blame the clothes. *If I try to look fat and am seen as fat, it is better than trying to be thin and failing.*"

Children steal, lie, use drugs, cut, starve, or skip school for many reasons, and to alleviate a variety of unwanted feelings and anxieties. But most often, what I hear from students is that they carry the enormous weight of the hopes and dreams their parents have for them—and the fears that they will be unable to fulfill those aspirations.

In wilderness therapy, assignments are given to help children learn why they do what they do. These assignments teach a principle or skill and are often given in the form of a letter. "The Benefits of Destructive Behaviors" letter helps them identify the needs that have been met by the behaviors that initially led to an intervention. Students struggle with this. In their new setting, they want to appear cured of their old problems; they don't want to discuss them. When I ask a marijuana user about the benefits of smoking pot, he'll often say, "I really didn't like pot all that much," even though he had been using it daily for a year before coming to the program. These protests almost always mask a fear that such an admission would lead to even more accountability, as well as shame about their self-destructive behavior. That accountability could then lead to others holding them accountable for their choices, and that's frightening for many of them. Exploring shame can lead to the exploration of needs and feelings they have been working to ignore and suppress in the first place.

There is an adage in recovery programs: "Talking about the purpose of drug use ruins it." If you begin to identify the escape with that which you're trying to escape, you ruin the "high" because it ceases to produce numbness or a distraction and instead reminds you why you are using. That is exactly why we must look underneath.

Some time ago, on separate phone calls, two parents tried to convince me of the other's brand of crazy. "She's an alcoholic," he demanded. "He's a borderline," she insisted. And each parent asked me if I saw it, wanting to make sure I was not getting fooled by the other. My response to both was this: "I can imagine your ex has a certain style of defending themselves. Our symptoms are organized into patterns we call diagnosis. Those are not very interesting to me. But what I would rather see and understand is the wound that leads to the symptoms. Finding that will be the most likely road to healing."

There are a couple of precautions to take when trying to understand the "why" of what your child is doing. Sometimes parents put boundaries aside in an attempt to understand their children's behaviors. If we can understand why a child is behaving in a certain way, perhaps consequences will not be necessary. In such cases, empathy robs accountability. This line of reasoning misses the idea that we can understand our children while still presenting them with consequences to their behavior. A wife can understand that her husband suffers from alcoholism and that he was genetically predisposed to having the disease while *also* taking care of herself. As a parent, I can set boundaries. The beauty of this stance is that the boundary comes not out of anger, but out of love for ourselves and others. These limits come from a place of compassion rather than judgment.

SHAPING BEHAVIORS

Another related principle is the concept of rewarding *successive approximations*. This is the idea of rewarding start behaviors, even if your child hasn't gotten something all the way right yet. This means giving your child a reward for taking steps in the right direction. The following story illustrates the concept of successive approximations through a humorous example.

In his biography of Steve Jobs, Walter Isaacson describes how Jobs created a remote control that could disrupt television signals. By rewarding successive approximations as people tried to adjust their sets to improve the picture, Jobs was able to get people to hold their antenna, stand on one foot, stand on the antenna, and bang it around to get their signals back. He influenced people to do almost anything he wanted them to do by shaping and rewarding their behaviors through successive approximations—engineering, behaviorally, what he wanted people to do.

EXTINCTION BURST: DON'T GIVE UP

Another important part of behavioral theory is the idea of an *extinction burst*. An extinction burst is the concept that when you stop rewarding behavior or start disincentivizing behavior, the negative behavior actually increases. For example, your child starts to beg and whine when you're checking out at the grocery store in order to get a candy bar.

When you first levy a tough consequence, you're often going to see an increase in the kinds of behaviors that led you to take a stronger

If you usually give in to behavior, and one day you do not, then you're going to see an escalation before the behavior stops.

stance. Your children are going to tell you they hate you; they are going to tell you they're not going to do well or learn anything, they don't love you and won't forgive you. Extinction bursts are natural but they're something we need to prepare for emotionally so we don't make premature judgments about whether the new limit or the new behavioral response is working.

Creating appropriate consequences. The first step to constructing a consequence is recognizing our boundaries. These represent the starting point in determining the limits we set with our children. When a parent can identify their own feelings and goals, they get much closer to seeing the child's needs clearly.

It is important to ensure that the consequence is *logical*—that it relates to the targeted behavior. If the only consequence you ever present your child is taking away their car, then that particular consequence may not always relate to the behavior in question and thus it might be difficult for your child to understand the message. If they get a speeding ticket, then you might need to take away the car. And if they stay out past their curfew, it may be more logical to withdraw the privilege of going out with friends that weekend.

You can also create positive consequences. If your child consistently comes home before their curfew, then you might increase their weekend privileges and let them stay out a little later on a Saturday. I once told my daughter, "You've earned the privilege of staying out later. I'm giving you the opportunity to do well or not do well. You've earned that." Presenting her with those consequences was initially difficult for her to accept because it placed the responsibility in her hands.

For many parents, the temptation is to rescue their child from the unpleasant aspects that result from their choices. This may seem to emanate from a place of love. But looking at the bigger picture we often realize that our rescuing behaviors are at cross-purposes with the long-term goals we want for our children. Many of the lessons that arise from failures or mistakes are very valuable. I am told that Jung would respond to his clients' promotions, achievements, and successes with the sentiment, "If we all stick together, we can get through this." Regarding their illnesses, divorces, and setbacks, he would offer, "Let's break open a bottle of champagne and celebrate."

As parents, we struggle at times to tolerate even mild suffering. Our children's suffering becomes our suffering. We feel inept and impotent when we can't provide them with a soft landing. But while this coddling may have been necessary when they were younger and more helpless, as they grow we need to grow and change with them. When it comes to our children's difficulties, we need to distinguish between mild and severe danger. It is important to allow our children to struggle and fail. If we don't make individual payments on our parenting plan along the way, so to speak, then we are often surprised to have to make a very painful and large balloon payment.

It is difficult not to fall into this trap with our children. We feel what they feel. So much of our identity is tied to their pain and their happiness. But it is critical to remember that it's okay for them to struggle and to experience pain.

Be careful of creating what I call a "hothouse flower" by protecting your child from natural consequences or easing off because you think they can't deal with it.

If your teenage son's clothes are dirty because he refuses to assist with laundry, then he wears dirty clothes. It's as simple as that. Now, of course, this does not mean that you don't set limits to protect your kids from severe dangers or risks. It doesn't mean that if your child protests going to school you let him skip and flunk out. It doesn't mean being disconnected and permissive. I am more and more convinced that we can let our children stumble through things and learn by their own experience, the lesson offered by mistakes. Manage your anxiety so you can allow them to experiment with autonomy and learn the related lessons that one only learns when they encounter consequences. There is only one way to find out what it feels like to walk into a wall. Learn to value this process and it will change your serenity and improve the quality of the relationship with your child.

Even in more serious situations, it may be wise to allow your child to suffer the natural consequences of his actions rather than intervene. Sometimes parents go to great lengths financially and legally to rescue their child. Part of that is a desire to be in control. Sometimes, though, you must say, "I'm not going to get in the way of this. If you have to go to jail to learn this lesson, then you might have to go to jail. If you are issued a fine, then you need to get a job and work to pay it off. This is your consequence, not mine."

Take your time to learn how to allow your child to experience consequences. Many of my worst parenting decisions were impulsive and emotionally generated because I was putting a lot of pressure on myself to "get it right." Learn to take time as a parent and think things through. Walk away to think about it. Sleep on it, if you have to. Release yourself from the pressure of having to have the right answer quickly.

The art of creating consequences does not come naturally to me. It's something I work on, and I'm better at it than I used to be. I take the time to ask myself the questions, "What is my intention? How much of this is about my emotion? Can I get that out of the way and put this into perspective? Can I take a time-out? Can I maintain a connection with my child while still being firm? Can I respond to my fears of disconnection? Can I be aware of what might get in the way of my consistency and my firmness?" I'm getting better at it all the time, although I don't know if I'll ever be done with that journey. My personal goal is to create a life for myself in which I can have a positive relationship with my child and provide a context that encourages him or her to be healthy. With that in mind first and foremost, I can take a step back and not act impulsively, fearfully, or in anger.

THE PARENT'S SELF-AWARENESS

Ideally, our behavioral responses rest on a foundation of understanding. That is to say, if we merely focus on changing problem behaviors, we may miss valuable information along the way. As I have already stated, the negative behavior problems we see are only the proverbial tip of the iceberg. Underneath is a wealth of information. I encourage parents to slow down before attempting to change their children's behavior. If we move too quickly toward behavior change, without examining what those behaviors are telling us, we and our children may not understand their emotions.

We also want to make sure that we understand ourselves and our motives. Focus on the message and the intention of the message rather than the outcome or the response. Ask questions such as, "Is this an insightful way to communicate?" "Have I done this thoughtfully, deliberately, and clearly?" "Have I kept my child's needs in mind, or am I satisfying some other agenda?" "Are my boundaries clear and consequences consistent?"

If we are actively engaged in keeping ourselves grounded by asking these questions, then we won't be as susceptible to the kind of triggers from our children that create blowups from kneejerk reactions.

When your child says, "You're an idiot," your response can be, "You have no idea how true that is!" If your child says, "You're not fair," go ahead and admit, "No, this isn't fair, not totally. You might be right." Then there's nothing your child can argue with or push back against. Trying to always be right is one of the weakest positions you can take as a parent. You're just human, and you're doing the best you can.

Your power as a parent comes not from being perfect, but from your thoughts, heart, love, prayers, meditation, and the healthy relationships you have in your life with other adults. Siegel and Hartzell say it this way, "Even if we have come to understand ourselves

Do the best that you can, and let go of trying to make everything perfect.

well, our children will still make their own journey through life. . . . Our role as parents serves to support our children's development, not guarantee its outcome."

Doesn't engaging in behaviorism create a power struggle by its nature? That can be one of the most misunderstood ideas about behavioral change. The goal as a parent is to let go while also delivering consistent consequences that communicate clear lessons. The key is to detach yourself from your children's responses. Whether or not they like your system, whether they respond positively and with gratitude, whether they subscribe to the philosophy behind why you've set things up the way you have—that's not your focus. Just be clear about your actions: "Here's my best attempt to communicate a clear, firm boundary and principle, and I'm going to let you do with it what you want. You can ignore it or reject it, rebel against it or go with it, but this is the way we're going to do it."

After one of my lectures, one parent said to me, "You say to let my daughter hate the consequence or hate me, as long as she is being respectful. Please explain how this can be respectful. The accusation of hate and respect, by definition, seem mutually exclusive."

Personally, I don't have an aversion to the word "hate," and I don't let it get to me. When my children tell me they hate me, my response is, "Okay." We want them to tell us how they feel. It doesn't do them or us any good to hide it from us. It is there whether they say it or not and I would like to be the one my child is talking to. You get to make the rules, but if it is about ego, you might consider the cost of restricting communication. Slamming doors, yelling at you, calling you names, using words or language you don't approve of—these are all examples of limits you can set; each parent's will be different.

INTERNALIZING CHANGE

We often make a mistake when we treat our children as little adults. They aren't. Their minds—and thus their capacity to think abstractly about the lessons we teach them—is still developing. I sometimes catch myself trying to reason with my preschool-aged child and my elementary-aged children as if they have the same brain capacity I do. Children learn differently. They learn by trial and error: finding out what works to get the results they want. From there, it takes years to develop a moral code and the psychological and cognitive sophistication of an adult.

Many parents resist using behavioral consequences because they fear they will not be helping their child develop an internal sense of right and wrong. But this perspective ignores the emotional and cognitive development of children. Morality begins with external consequences and only gradually moves internally, through maturation and experience.

As a parent, you can only control your own actions—the way that you act toward your children and the things that you try to teach them. You can't control whether or not they actually listen or implement those lessons into their lives. Their lives are their own, really.

Of course, letting your children walk their own paths doesn't make you uninvolved, disconnected, or permissive. It just means that you recognize they have to figure it out for themselves. All you can do is communicate your messages and values as clearly and consistently as you can. Every child will stumble, including yours. But the more they trust you, the more likely they will come to you when they are struggling, stuck, or in danger.

Allowing our children to have their journey comes, in part, when we recognize our own journey. And when we embrace all the aspects of our own path, we learn to value the struggle and setbacks, not just the triumphs.

Don't obsess over whether your children have internalized your values. It is impossible to know. Remain firm and clear with your boundaries, but try to take your emotion out of the situation. In doing so, you'll become less angry and reactive. This is not to say that you won't have feelings. You're their parent! You will continue to feel passionately about their mistakes and their triumphs. Just don't let those feelings cause you to lose your own footing.

Recently, a parent asked me, "How do I get my eight-year-old son to realize that helping out around the house is part of what it means to be a part of our family? He will participate, but his attitude isn't one of contribution but rather of obligation." My answer was simple: "You don't. You don't try to control what he thinks or feels." On the contrary, a parent could even go so far as to empathize with the drudgery of chores, about how he might rather be doing something fun too. Children, especially young children, don't learn the way adults do. They learn by repetition, by doing. They learn concretely, rather than through abstract lectures.

OUR CHILDREN LEARN FROM THE OUTSIDE IN

How do children learn? The answer is often from the outside in rather than through epiphanies. We adults lecture; we debate. I found myself arguing with my preschool-aged child some time ago about wearing shoes when leaving the house before I came to my senses and said out loud, "I am debating with a four-year-old and I think she is winning."

You are living and dying by the same sword. Every time you try to prove you are right, your child finds another issue to fight against. Don't focus on getting your child to *believe* that something is right, and don't make subscribing to your beliefs among your expectations.

The minute you get into a debate with your child about right and wrong, about what should be thought or felt, is the minute you lose.

Instead, set up a system where you say, "Here's the behavior and here's the consequence. This is the positive and this is the negative. *You* get to decide what you think and how you feel about this. I'm not going to try to convince you of anything, I'm simply going to attach myself to executing this plan."

Imagine somebody came to you and said, "My son has gone over the allotted amount of minutes on his cell phone for the last three months. I have talked to him about it each month, but it keeps happening." What would you say to that parent? You would probably say, "Take away his cell phone" or "Make him work to earn the money in order to pay you back." You would suggest stopping the insanity of just trying to talk the son into using his cell phone responsibly. The only way he's going to learn is if there's a concrete consequence.

We can be misled by the belief that our children will want to do a particular thing based on its own intrinsic merit. By examining the development of young adult and adolescent children, we are reminded that this is *not* the way they learn. Instead, they learn through experience, through consequence: the world rewards certain behaviors and punishes certain behaviors. As adults we are more abstract in our thinking, and so we want our children to learn similarly. We want them to have an epiphany, and then change their patterns. But that's not usually how it works with young people.

A few years ago, I worked with an incredibly bright young man whose IQ was in the 99th percentile, but his behavior was driving his parents crazy. They too were bright, but eventually in any given situation he would outlast and outwit them with his lies and manipulation. Early in treatment I too was impressed with the young man's verbal ability. But there was something missing. He could rationalize and intellectualize, but he couldn't feel or connect. Several of our early sessions ended abruptly due to my belief that he wasn't ready to talk about what was really going on with him. These abbreviated sessions left him extremely frustrated, as did the assignment for extended self-reflection interventions that I tasked him with.

Our spirited debates were not what he needed, and I wasn't going to convince him of that any more than his parents had already. After a great deal of time his ability to engage and be authentic did improve. It was a slow process but by the end of his course of stay in wilderness therapy, he had become much more genuine—he had found himself in certain ways. On the last day of our program, his mother shared with me this realization: "The most important thing I learned from your program is that children learn from the outside in. I have been spending all my energy trying to talk my child into healthy behavior, trying to make him understand. I was seduced by our talks. But now I have learned to walk away from those intoxicating discussions. God knows I love to hear myself speak, but that is not how my son learns."

GUILTING

As children ourselves, many of us were guilted by our parents. We were told to feel bad, or at least it was implied, when we did something to upset them. If this is true for you, do you remember how it made you feel?

Teach your child they are not responsible for your feelings. Keep the conversations short and avoid the temptation to lecture. You may express your feelings, but make them about you and not about the child. This is called owning your emotions, something very few people do.

It is easy to use praise or criticism as reinforcement but it can lead to shame and poor differentiation. A father of a child in our wilderness program described the following scenario during a parent meeting. He had asked his son for help in moving some things into his office on a Saturday morning, and his son refused. "I am really, really disappointed in you," the father had told his son. Several of the other parents at the meeting encouraged this father by saying things like "Great job!" I took a step back and I said to this dad, "What was your goal in saying it that way?" His answer was, "Well, I wanted him to change."

Here it is important to remember that our disappointment is *our* problem, not our child's. It's something that they can be made aware of, but it's not their job to make us happy. It's *your* job to make yourself happy. Our emotions can help us understand what's going on in our lives, but it's not our children's responsibility to recognize that and to change their own to make us happy. A healthier statement may have been, "I'm sad you don't want to help me, and will have to deal with your decision somehow."

DON'T THEY HAVE TO WANT TO CHANGE?

Ultimately, yes, people have to want to change in order to change. But part of our job as parents is creating motivation for that change—offering the child a proverbial carrot so that they might work toward a healthy goal is a primary parental responsibility.

A colleague of mine worked in a parent-coaching program. In this program, which usually follows some form of residential treatment for the child, the parent is assigned a coach and the child is assigned a mentor. After running this program for years, my colleague observed the following phenomenon. There are basically three classes of families he sees: First, both the child and parents are motivated. Those tend to be successful. Second, neither the child nor the parent is motivated. They have very little success avoiding problems and relapses with these families. But the third class, which he referred to as "chasers," describes parents who are motivated and a child who is not—at least not intrinsically. Incredibly, they have the same success rate with the chasers as they do in the cases where both the child and the parents are motivated. This observation is very similar to the one I have concluded in my career, which is supported in the literature of Joanna Bettmann, a researcher in the field of wilderness therapy. She reported that a client's desire or readiness for change was not related to significant therapeutic improvement.

Lessons from Behavioral Contracts

A common tool for dealing with a child's behavioral problems is to create a contract where the rules are clearly laid out with corresponding consequences and privileges. Many parents hope that the negotiated, agreed-upon, and signed behavioral contracts will ensure success.

Rarely (or never) after violating the behavioral contract does the child approach the parent and admit, "Yep. I screwed up. I deserve the consequence. I just wanted to let you know that I get it." Rather, they are likely to debate loopholes and suggest that the contract was signed under duress. Don't think for a moment that the contract alone is enough; you will be required to continue to enforce limits and to take on all the responsibility and associated heartache that comes with that process for it to be successful. Creating a contract provides the parent with a tool that facilitates clarity and helps crystallize one's philosophy and intentionality, which can help the parent feel confident in standing up to the child: it is in black and white. It can also release the parent from self-doubt. ("Maybe I wasn't clear on this with her.") But if you expect the contract will do the work for you, and that your child will not fight back when the contract needs to be enforced, that is wishful thinking. You will still need to be the bad guy.

Once I was talking with a mother who was struggling with her son's regression after graduating from our program some months earlier. Her son had violated just about everything in his behavioral contract. She was incredulous. "Doesn't he remember all the lessons he learned? I know I am not supposed to yell and lecture," she admitted, "but I had to go up to his room yesterday and ask him why he would do the same old things!" I gently pointed out the irony of what she had just told me, "So you went up to his room to engage in the same old behaviors that you know aren't healthy for you, to ask him why he was behaving in the same old ways that he knows aren't healthy for him?" She paused and chuckled at herself. We can become so obsessed with our children's behaviors and their problems that we miss the mark when it comes to ourselves.

Understanding Crazy

Part of our inability to understand our children may be that they are manifesting something about us that we have not yet made peace with ourselves. It may be a part of us we discarded a long time ago, some characteristic we no longer manifest; however, discarding it is not the same as making peace with it. When our children invite us to look at our split-off parts and we say, "I don't understand you," what we actually mean is that we don't want to see it in our children because if we did, it would terrify us. Our constant questioning, "Why are you doing this?" is really "Please stop, you are hurting me, frustrating me, or scaring me."

One barrier that prevents many parents from moving forward is realizing that it may not be healthy or even possible to understand some irrational types of behavior. For example, we might have a loved one who struggles with severe mental illness or addiction, and their experiences may be beyond our rational ability to understand. However, as parents we more commonly see our children suffering from the "disease of childhood." At times, this "disease" renders children incapable of rational thought and prevents them from seeing the connection between cause and effect, or from understanding how the future relates to their current behavior. Then you, the parent, will be in a state of disbelief and will inevitably ask, "Why did you do that?" The child's answer of "I don't know" is an honest, albeit unsatisfying, response.

A few years ago, my four children sat eating at the dinner table. Isabella, who was seven at the time, was eager to share some of her new-found knowledge of science with the family. She looked at my son Jake, then sixteen years old, and said, "I know why you are sometimes not nice to me. My teacher said you are missing the front part of your brain and that makes it so you are not always thinking right." After a few chuckles from the table, Jake retorted, "Yeah, well you're missing that part of your brain too!"

They were both right, and the lesson is this: the executive part of the brain—the part of the brain that is rational and logical—is not fully developed in the average person until his or her mid-to-late twenties.

Children operate from a more primitive part of the brain, so our treating them like "little" adults is poorly matched.

Neurologically, their brains lack some of the structure it requires to comprehend and retain the kind of reasoning that adults can master.

Parents are often eager to pinpoint a particular event that may have led to the child's current behavioral problems. "Was it the adoption? Was it the divorce? Is it parental conflict, peer conflict, or sibling conflict?" They want a clear, clean, and simple explanation. They believe that if they can just get that answer, then they can manage their child's behavior. However, the goal is not for you to manage his behavior. The goal is to teach him to address his feelings, to understand them, and to see how they affect him. With behavioral management techniques, we cut off easy access to escape routes, shortcuts, and dead ends by instead providing tools for feelings that can be employed in the long term.

Teaching children how to feel provides the tools necessary for them to discover the roots of their difficulties. Armed with those tools, it becomes the child's job to acknowledge his feelings and tell us why he is doing what he is doing. And of course, like many of us, our children will discover different versions or explanations for themselves as they progress through life. So when a parent asks me the question "Why is my child acting in this crazy way?" sometimes I simply respond by saying, "I truly don't know. I have some good ideas, and we will explore the usual suspects, but, most importantly, we are going to help your child find the answer to that question himself." Adapting the old adage "Teach a man to fish . . . " is more important than you or a therapist catching the fish for him.

HOW DO I KNOW IF THIS IS NORMAL TEENAGE BEHAVIOR OR SOMETHING MORE SERIOUS?

This is one of the most difficult and frustrating questions for a parent to consider. If a parent consults with therapists, child psychologists, and other parents, they may find contradictory responses. These contradictions add to a parent's feeling of hopelessness, and they may eventually conclude, "No one has an answer. Even the experts we have consulted don't agree." So, as is the theme of this book, I would like to suggest a different source for finding the answer—*you*. I want to share a way of thinking that allows you to find an answer within yourself that will bring hope, optimism, and a sense of liberation.

Some time ago, a father approached me and described his dilemma. His nineteen-year-old son was living at home and smoking some pot. He was otherwise cooperative, although his motivation, organization, and ambition were limited. The father began to ask me for facts, for studies, for ammunition to show his son the detrimental effects of marijuana, even when used in moderation. He described how they had debated the effects of marijuana and how his son had a plethora of facts to support his position that occasional use was harmless. I responded by encouraging the father to explain to his son that he could continue to smoke pot if he did not believe it was harmful, but that he could not continue to smoke it in his father's home.

"Is that enough?" the father asked. In essence, he was asking, "Am *I* enough?"

"Yes," I responded with certainty. You can't prove to your child that you are right. You can quote theorists, experts, studies, or even God, and your son can rebut with his own expert witnesses. A much more powerful and unassailable stance is to give an "I" statement: "I don't believe . . . I don't want . . . I feel . . . I think . . ." If we don't do this, we are in danger of conveying the need to be right. While you can argue the merits or objective reality of a position, there is no realistic argument against an "I think" statement. I even encourage parents to take this a step further and state, "*I might be wrong*, but this is my belief or experience."

In his book *Nonviolent Communication: A Language of Life*, Marshall B. Rosenberg explains that when we express our thoughts or feelings as being right, we are suggesting that the other person's thoughts or feelings are wrong. He explains that when expressing our feelings and needs using "I" statements, we are less likely to evoke defensiveness or trigger a debate. In the end, if you tell your nineteen-year-old son that you might be wrong and maybe even an idiot, he will likely not argue in response.

In the spirit of what works, let's go back to this question: "Is this normal, or is this just a phase or a stage?" Talking to psychologists, therapists, and other parents will help to give you a reference point. These individuals can share their experiences with you; they can share what they see in their own practice. This can be useful, but it doesn't mean you have to do it their exact way. I often say to people, "Here is what I see, but understand that my frame of reference is a very unique one."

There is another way to consider "normal" development: by asking, "Is this ideal?" While none of us may ever achieve the ideal, it is still something for which we can strive.

Instead of deciding what is "normal," figure out what you want for yourself and your kids, what you like, what you believe, and what you think is ideal, and work toward that.

A focus of mine as a parent educator is to liberate parents to act assertively and confidently while still maintaining a sense of openness and humility. It is possible to feel empowered while still leaving yourself open to learning and listening opportunities. Defending or justifying your parenting decisions, especially to your child, is not empowered parenting. I often illuminate this by referencing the following quote by Henry T. Close:

There is no question but that our parents failed us as parents. All parents fail their children, and ours were no exception. No parent is ever adequate enough for the job of being a parent, and there is no way not to fail at it. No parent ever has enough love, or wisdom, or maturity, or patience. No parent ever succeeds

completely. . . . We must forgive them for our sake, not theirs . . .
in order for us to be really free to find other sources of parenting,
we must forgive.

When I first started working with students in wilderness therapy, I
listened to them complain about their "idiot" parents. Initially, I saw
myself as a sort of detective or judge. I would hear stories from other
members in the family and then decide where the faults lay. After a
while, I realized that this approach was futile. There was no perfect parent. The complaints, hurts, and wounds expressed by the children were
not necessarily an indictment of the parents. Those feelings were real,
but they existed at that moment in time, and they changed and evolved
as time went on.

When you are trying to explain your correctness about a particular
parenting decision to your child, you are merely exposing your own
insecurity.

And where a parent falls short, it will be up to *A truly secure*
her child to make the difference. I am always amazed *parent does not*
to see the parents I deal with put blame on them- *need to know that*
selves for their children's struggles. Yet those same *she is perfect, but*
parents tend not to blame *their* mistakes on their *rather can be*
parents. You can't have it both ways! *comfortable with*

Perhaps an even greater limitation of showing *her limitations.*
that we are "right" is that need we have for our kids to
agree with us and our decisions. If we win the debate and prove that we
are right, we tell ourselves, then they will not be angry with us and we
won't have to do the difficult work of setting a boundary without the
approval of our children. This is a common Achilles' heel for almost all
parents I come into contact with, whether or not they are dealing with
struggling children. I came across an article from the satirical publication
The Onion that demonstrates this principle of "liberated parenting":

A study released by the California Parenting Institute Tuesday shows that every style of parenting inevitably causes children to grow into profoundly unhappy adults. Despite great variance in parenting styles across populations, the end product is always the same: a profoundly flawed and joyless human being.

When my son was in eighth grade, I received a call from his school. He was sick and would not respond to questions, and they wanted permission to call an ambulance if they could not deal with the situation on campus. I, of course, told them that it was, and rushed to the school immediately. I arrived ten minutes later and was greeted by the vice principal. He was standing outside the boys' restroom and informed me that my son had admitted to drinking a soda bottle filled with rum. He was vomiting and crying on the floor of the restroom, pleading with me to believe that he had learned his lesson.

I took him to the emergency room, where he was admitted for possible alcohol poisoning. I was told that in such cases parents were legally required to meet with a hospital social worker. When the social worker arrived, she explained that my son had consumed a large amount of alcohol but that he would be fine. She explained to me the importance of supervising children with vigilance. "You need to have conversations about drinking and drugs," she said. After listening to her exhortations on the effective parenting of an at-risk adolescent, I told her my profession. I told her we had sent our son to a wilderness program—my wilderness program—for four months after an episode where he drank alcohol at a neighbor's house. I told her that I had the best drug tests on the market, and that I administered them randomly. I had purchased the finest retail version of an alcohol Breathalyzer that I could find. I called homes where he was hanging out. I organized neighborhood groups in our community in which parents could talk about common issues with our children and share resources about drug and alcohol use. I told her that my son was in therapy—

that we were in therapy together. Defensively, I said that maybe that's why he had been drinking in school, because if he did it after school then I would have caught him.

After my condescending diatribe on my "supervision philosophy" with my son, the social worker calmly responded, "You need to back off. Your son needs some freedom." Huh? So which was it? She gave her initial speech on supervision when she assumed I was an uninvolved parent, and when I explained my approach, she told me to back off. While I think her initial assessment and canned lecture to me was off track, she did highlight an important point: it wasn't about me always getting it right. Is it common for adolescents to experiment with drinking, getting into trouble, and making really poor choices? Yes. My job is strictly to do the best I can without believing that if I get everything perfect I could prevent a phase or problem from occurring.

Parents often approach me to ask whether or not the problems they are experiencing with their children are severe enough to warrant an out-of-home intervention. One gauge I have found helpful is to ask parents, "Can your child still be part of the solution? Is the child willing to talk, willing to respond to consequences in the home?" Therapy, family meetings in which healthy communication is achieved, and reasonable responsiveness to consequences are all evidence that a child is moving forward. It is never an easy course to work with someone who is struggling—there are often two steps forward, then many steps back. Broken contracts and empty promises are common responses to parental attempts to address problem behaviors. Even when raising "typical" teens, parents will experience setbacks. And if they come to an impasse time and again, then yes, maybe it's a good idea to take the solution outside of the home. The key is for the parent to do all that they feel they can do. Coercing a parent with fear or guilt to "do the right thing" will often result in a loss of steam, a wavering of resolve, or a subsequent abandonment of a serious intervention when it is needed. You, the parent, need to feel that the decision is right for you and your child.

Another way to think about the question of whether or not the behavior of your child warrants further help is this:

An early intervention is better than a late one.

As previously stated, we strive for an ideal rather than striving to be normal. We go to the gym and work toward a toned body that very few of us ever achieve. We attend church, listen to scholarly lectures, or read inspiring books, never reaching the heights of virtue set forth in those arenas. But we can always work toward them. Our ability to do this and to forgive ourselves for falling short is what leads to a healthier and happier life.

When you offer an intervention for your child that you believe is lifesaving, or at least life-enhancing, is it the right choice? I don't know. You could find professionals or other parents to support either position. In the end, you will need to go with your gut and make your own choice as the parent of your child. Then you need to own that choice. When you own your choices as a parent—and your feelings and beliefs and perspectives—you clear the way for your child to take responsibility for their own choices.

So is your child's behavior "normal"? Here are some essential questions to consider:

How do you feel?

What do you want in your home?

What do you want to communicate to your child about your values through the boundaries you will set?

What is your intention?

Is what you feel "good enough"?

Will you allow your child to disagree and dislike you?

Can you let go of being right and understand that you are good enough to make the decision?

Can you turn the responsibility over to your child to let them grow up, forgive, resist, resent, or otherwise make of it what they choose?

Remember, our children can grow up, despite our limitations. When we turn this responsibility over to them, we are showing them, "I have confidence that you can overcome my failings." And if we are to blame for how our children turn out, that's okay. We, in turn, can blame our own parents for raising us so poorly!

YOU ARE NOT OFF COURSE

Perhaps the most important contribution of heroic parenting is the idea that we embrace our journey rather than become a victim to it.

Many of the parents I see whose children are struggling are authentically grieving the loss of "normal family life" and the typical milestones and rites of passage that families experience in raising young adult and teenage children. I honor that grief. Yet many parents also experience an acute frustration and resentment toward the life they are being drawn into because of their child's choices. Loss of time and leisure, stress, fear, anxiety, attending court dates and therapy programs, and less time and energy available for the other children in the home— all these factors can lead to impatience and an unquenchable desire to return to a normal life.

Blame, complaints, and laments about the difficult journey may leave us unable to see the gifts raising a struggling child has to offer.

When parents attend my education groups, in every phase of the process, I often start with the following invitation: "Consider yourself on course. Even if it's just for the duration of the meeting, consider the possibility that this is exactly where you need to be, doing exactly what you need to be doing."

Several years ago I sat on the forest floor with a mother, father, and their seventeen-year-old son. It was near the end of their family visit. As I began the session and reviewed how the day had gone for each member of the family, his mother started with a story. Recently, though her son was away in the program, she attended a Senior Day football game. The custom was to call all the senior players' mothers down to the field, where their sons gave them a rose and a blanket with the player's number and letter sewn onto it. It was a touching show of gratitude for the sacrifices the mothers had made over the four years of their sons' football careers. As the mother began her story, I thought I knew where she was going and prepared myself to offer support and validation for her loss of this rite of passage. Then she surprised me by saying, "I felt so sorry for the other mothers and sons who were there that night because they are not getting the experience of getting to know their sons in the same way that we are. This experience has allowed us all to become so much closer." That sentiment, so sweetly communicated by this mother, is common among the families whose children we treat. "This problem has become one of life's greatest blessings," so many say. Rather than fixating on what should be or what is normal, embracing your individual journey can allow for happiness and fulfillment.

A story from my own family illustrates the same principle from a different perspective. My daughter Emma, fifteen years old at the time, approached me for an assignment in school titled "Job Shadow Day." Emma is a very successful student who almost never has trouble with teachers or with her mother and me. For her assignment, she was to pick a parent and follow them at work for a day, then present the experience to her class. I thought the richest experience I could give her was to take her out to the wilderness to visit a therapy group. Emma was excited but nervous.

Upon our arrival, the staff greeted us and we made our plans for the day. Among the nine girls in the group, there were issues of self-harm, eating disorders, sexual promiscuity, and mood disorders. Indeed, their struggles stood in sharp contrast to the life my daughter Emma was leading. We sat in a circle around the fire in an area cleared of snow and asked the girls to introduce themselves, sharing in their own words what had brought them to this point in their lives. (The exercise serves both as a way to introduce oneself as well as to assist the participants in clarifying their issues and goals.) Each girl told her story with a raw honesty and insight.

The introductions presented an easy transition to the group topic I had prepared. I read an excerpt about forgiveness and parenting to highlight to the girls that they all had imperfect parents and that forgiving their parents for that would be liberating for them. During the session, several of the girls participated actively and were able to relate to how they were stuck in a cycle of blame and victimization.

On the short walk back to the truck at the end of the day, I casually asked Emma what she thought of the visit. With an animated response, she talked about how impressed she was with the girls. "Their insight and ability to speak so clearly, honestly, and openly about themselves was amazing." Reflecting on her answer, I thought about how I would not want to trade Emma's problems with any of those girls. However, they were traveling a path that would offer them an education that would be difficult to replicate in Emma's life. Yes, Emma was and is successful by most accounts, but sometimes what initially seems like a detour from the one's path is the actual journey itself. That pain carves out a place within us and creates a place for greater joy and understanding of others and ourselves. So if you find yourself feeling like you're off track, consider this:

You might be right where your need to be, doing exactly what you need to be doing at this moment in time.

If we fail to embrace, no matter how painful or scary, the journey of parenting a struggling child, we will also miss the treasure that journey has to offer. For me, parenting struggling children offers many gifts, including increased compassion for others who suffer, clarity in recognizing our boundaries, and improved self-care.

CONCLUSION

How we think about our children is more important than what we do to them. The quality of an intervention or a behavioral technique is not as important as how we hold our children in our mind. If we see them as bad, broken, or sick, it doesn't matter what we *do*. Our anxiety will leak out subtly, and all they will see is that we think they are bad. It is critical that we learn to see them and their goodness, even when their behavior makes this difficult. If they sense that we are embarrassed or ashamed of them, they will absorb that negative energy and realize that our behavior is not coming from a place of love. This dynamic is exactly the reason why I encourage parents to frame their child's acting out in pragmatic terms. Will this behavior prevent them from leading a happy and successful life in the long term or not?

We can use behavioral interventions to nurture, guide, teach, and encourage our children. But we must also do our own work to make sure we are attending to the needs of the child. Sometimes, we listen to what they are *not* able to say and provide them comfort. To do this we follow the trail of crumbs back home to find the child. And there we offer them company and warmth and they heal themselves.

My last exhortation on this subject is that even if you do have the right tools to influence your child's behavior, do not move too quickly toward changing it. If you do, there is a risk that you and the child will miss the lesson the behavior is intended to teach both of you.

CHAPTER SIX

CONTROL VS. INFLUENCE

To the extent you try to control your children, you fail at influencing them.

—Paul E. Goddard, PhD

MANY YEARS AGO I WORKED FOR A COMPANY THAT USED the tagline "Let's fix the kids." The motto, and its package of step-by-step solutions, appealed to a lot of parents. Today, I hear similar phrases used in various advertisements about in-person and online seminars that promise that *you can change your child's behavior in just a few short weeks after watching this amazing symposium!* Imagine if we saw advertisements for seminars that promoted how to change your spouse, your friends, or your parents. I think very few of us would be tempted by that hollow promise. Yet for some reason it is very easy to believe that we can change our children. Of course, while they are young and more impressionable, we have a more significant impact on them. Yet thinking of children in this way is dangerous. It works at cross-purposes with our goal to allow children to develop healthily and become responsible for their own lives.

A consultant who had referred several cases to me told me, "Brad, talk to parents about looking inside of themselves, talk to them about doing their own work, but don't tell them that this is going to make their kids change." If I were to give a presentation to a group of parents on "How to Change your Child"—even if that presentation was full of good parenting techniques—then I'd really just be perpetuating the same faulty thinking that you can have ultimate control over somebody else.

A key task of growing into adulthood is to move from the victim's posture to a posture of empowerment. As children mature, they come to realize that their problems are not their parents' fault. Indeed, adolescence is the time of transitioning from "It's my parents' fault" to "It's mine to own." This transition becomes a rite of passage for the students and parents in our wilderness program. It does not sweep under the rug the hurts, shortcomings, and grief of childhood, but rather allows those experiences to pass through the child. Through this process, a child may fully feel each wound, great or small, and can integrate them into a more whole self, one filled with a sense of liberation, joy, and compassion.

This chapter details the ways in which parents can facilitate this process. It will also debunk some myths about control as well as some common errors parents make. Ultimately, it will address the forces that drive us toward and away from the path of control.

TWO CONTINUUMS

The following model depicts different styles of parenting. We begin with the principle that permissiveness and strictness are not on the same continuum as controlling and influential parenting. You can be controlling and permissive or controlling and strict. You can also be influential and permissive or influential and strict. Strictness or permissiveness is *not* a measure of our level of control. Most of us think controlling and strict exist on one end and permissive and influential on the other. I constructed this diagram with two axes because I've seen it in action. And when strict parents let go of their control over the outcome, they are able to maintain their rules and standards but let their children experience the consequences of their actions. They can let their children be angry or upset with them without feeling tied to that response.

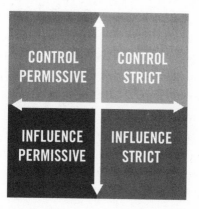

Your child might say, "I'm never going to talk to you again if you give me this consequence." But if you are coming from a well-grounded perspective, you will know how to respond—try something like, "Well, I guess I'm going to have to live with that, but I'm still going to do this because I think it's best for you." If your child can't forgive you, that's his problem, not yours. Healthy people forgive their parents, eventually, for all that they do. What's important is that you, as a parent, understand the difference between trying to exert control over your child and setting clear boundaries.

I don't usually give a lot of specific advice about how strict to be—that part is up to you. What I promote is instruction on how to align your parenting boundaries, limits, and values in a clear way so that you can experience liberation and agility. Is it right to set a boundary on cigarettes for a child recovering from drug addiction? Should you let

Though it's tempting to ask the "experts" for advice and clarification about what is "normal," the answer is inside you.

them hang around friends who might be a bad influence on them? I can't answer that. I'll talk to you about reasoning, risks, and ways to manage behaviors. I'll ask you questions about your intentions. But *you* must decide the rules.

The answers are inside all of us, but can be blocked by fear and self-doubt. And this creates a disconnect from yourself and your child. Focus on discovering confidence in your choices rather than which particular line in the sand you draw.

What are your boundaries? What level of structure are you comfortable with? From there, communicate your thoughts and feelings assertively, consistently, and in a manner that makes it clear to the child that it is not their responsibility to take care of your feelings. The next step is to establish a plan with your child about rules, rewards, and related consequences. Don't assume you have all the answers—just *your* answers. Let your child make her choice and deal with the consequences. Remain confident that either path they take will provide the lesson they need.

Clarity is its own reward. When you achieve clarity, you are in the right frame of mind to create a healthy situation for yourself and those around you. I know that I can allow my children to be angry and upset with me, but I strive not to stray from my course and my truth. With others in my life, I find my center as best I can and choose my course; the others get to decide if they want to stay connected and stay in my life.

An important question to ask yourself is, "What is in the way of me knowing my truth?" There is where your work lies.

The things that obscure our truth and our paths are the voices that tell us we are not okay. When we can learn to confront those voices and dispel them from our minds, then we can walk our path—even if it is a little frightening. We walk it because we know it is *ours*.

WHAT IS CONTROL?

Let's examine the Serenity Prayer. It's customary for twelve-step groups to close their meetings with this prayer, and it adds context to our discussion about control. The prayer reads:

> *God, grant me the serenity to accept the things I cannot change,*
> *The courage to change the things I can,*
> *And the wisdom to know the difference.*

There is a pretty simple distinction here. What can we change? We can change ourselves and our reactions. What can't we change? Everything else. We can influence and have an impact on other people, but the idea that we can do both—change ourselves *and* control others—is nothing but an intoxicating illusion.

Exerting control over somebody else gives you a false sense of power. Authentic power, on the other hand, lies in changing *yourself.* It's the "wisdom to know the difference"—to be able to "accept the things I cannot change." If you learn how to do this, you will feel genuine power, and it will truly change your life. A maxim from *The Parent's Handbook: Systematic Training for Effective Parenting (STEP)* suggests the greatest challenge in parenting teens is to focus on changing yourself, not your teenager. Redirecting this focus changes the parent from hopeless to hopeful, powerless to powerful, and from victim to a free agent in one's own life.

Of course, my temptation, like many of yours, is still to try to manipulate people. What can I say? I'm a therapist. My job is, in a sense, to professionally manipulate. I too have a hard time reminding myself that I can't change people—and they don't need my changing. Of course, one of my students or one of my own children will inevitably come along and remind me that I am not in control of him or her—and I thank them for that. I'll say, "Thanks for reminding me that I am only in control of myself. It's people like you that give me that gift, and I'm really grateful for that."

INFLATED PARENTING

Many parents are outwardly successful in a variety of ways—they're charismatic, they have a talent for motivating people, they are high achievers in their careers, they are powerful leaders. If you are successful in any of these ways, it is understandable that you possess confidence and believe that you can change others. It is also understandable that you apply the same skills that made you successful in these other spheres to your new task of parenthood. You look at your child and think, "It's my job to make you happy and successful."

Remember that your child comes with his or her own will. The responsibility of the parent is to be present, aware, loving, and intentional. But always keep in mind . . . you'll fail at this on a daily basis. I've said to my family on many occasions, "There is a list of things I failed at today. I got a lot of things accomplished, but there are a lot of things on my list that I didn't do." The difference between good and bad self-esteem isn't having a sense of your great qualities. It's making peace with your limitations. The goal here is how to become an effective parent. In order to do that, we must make the conceptual distinction between controlling our children and having an influence and impact on them.

The trick is to let go of the idea of holding yourself responsible for your children while still holding yourself responsible for what you do.

By holding yourself responsible for your child's reactions, successes, and emotions, you are essentially making that child feel smaller and smaller. That is, if you consider yourself the cause and effect of everything, you'll contribute to your child's belief that everything in the world is somebody else's fault.

I understand it's counterintuitive to separate your behavior from your child's. It just takes practice. When making a parenting decision, try to stop thinking about how your child will react and just speak from your heart. Focus on what you want to communicate and express. Your child's successes and failures are theirs; your failures and success are yours. We can acknowledge and recognize our impact on our children without taking away their sense of self or choice to react a certain way.

THE COINCIDENCE OF GOOD PARENTS AND GOOD KIDS

Even if the only reason you are willing to try some of these principles is because you think it might have a positive outcome on your child, that's okay. I understand that's always going to be part of the motivation. I still believe good parenting is its own reward but I don't discount the incentive of positively impacting your child. What I try to avoid, however, is talking to people about being "good" parents in the context of raising "good" children. The two things are separate and I discourage this harmful and objectifying cause-and-effect thinking in parents.

Parenting is more than just a means to an end. If you are willing to participate in this process; if you are ready to look at what you can do to become a better communicator; if you are open to becoming a more effective, intentional, thoughtful, and creative parent; if you can respond to your child in a way that's more empowered and less reactive; and if you can learn how to define your boundaries clearly, then you will be guided by these principles.

It is humility that invites our children to open up and be vulnerable. They need and want us to travel our own journey. I recently began working with a family on better listening techniques, and the father insisted, "We *are* good listeners. We have

But if you are secretly waiting for someone to give you that magic button you can push that will change your child, then I can't help you.

always listened well to our son." But during the following weeks of family therapy, he changed his tune: "I have learned that I am not a very good listener," he said. "I thought I was listening, but it was only my agenda that I paid attention to. And realizing that I struggle with listening to my son is something that is bringing us together." All our children need from you is an attitude that tells them, "I am sorry for my mistakes. I am not perfect and struggle at times; my struggle is mine—not yours." Not only is effective parenting its own reward, as I often state, but effective and healthy parenting *is* effective and healthy living.

EMOTIONAL COERCION

Controlling parenting is emotionally coercive parenting. Healthy parenting, on the other hand, is about, first becoming aware of your own internal processes, meanings, beliefs, and feelings. Second is developing this awareness so you can share your true self with your child. This is the ultimate goal. Your kids can adapt to any level of structure. What they will struggle with is adjusting to an emotionally controlling and coercive environment. That is a ball and chain that they are going to want to discard immediately.

I have sat in on countless sessions between a parent and a child in which the child has grumbled about a decision the parent has made. The parent will in turn ask, "Okay, how do I fix that?" To which I reply, "You don't fix it. It is not broken. You *listen* to it."

I was running a parent support meeting recently, in which a father and mother were sharing their angst regarding their young adult son.

This impulse to manage or fix our child's feelings is where most parents go off course.

He had made some progress over the last few years, but seemed to have hit a rough patch. I know these parents well—they are loving, caring, and compassionate. They do their work and "get it," but the nature of their son's disease would pull anyone toward a dark place.

In our Q&A session, the father said, "I am practicing listening and it just doesn't seem to work. The more I try to use the skills, the more frustrated my son gets. I listen, reflect, and walk away when I need to set a boundary. No matter what I do, he still accuses me of trying to control his feelings. And I really am just listening, but nothing seems to change his perception." So I responded, illustrating for the group, "Do you see what Dan is doing? Dan is the most loving and sincere control freak I know." Dan's eyebrows rose. I asked him, "Why is it not okay that your son is still upset? Why is it that he has to get over his feelings? It sounds like he is right. You *do* want to control what he feels. Yes, this comes from a place of compassion, but you are still trying to change how he feels and he can sense you doing that. So his accusations, in some way, are true." Dan nodded in understanding and we all acknowledged how easily we can get lost in the process.

The intricacies of guilt and shame are addressed later in the book, but it is important to state here that these most often lead to emotionally coercive parenting. Our children are still developing their moral maturity, so moralizing to them is like trying to teach a six-year-old algebra: it doesn't work. For most children, their maturation and brain development will simply not allow it. So stop thinking in terms of right and wrong.

It is far more effective when we simply model morality in our own behavior and actions. We can also teach morality by setting boundaries but not by lecturing or shaming.

Moralizing with children invites a power struggle because the essence of identity is finding and defining one's own way and values.

A lot of times kids react defensively toward me, as if I am a moral authority. I'm not; I am a guide who knows some helpful skills and tools. I say, "I'm not your priest. I'm not your pastor or rabbi, probation officer, or a cop. I'm a therapist. This isn't about me, it's about you. I'll care about you if you'll let me, but this isn't about my life. If I make my practice about your life, I am screwed."

Therapists who make their life about their clients quickly burn out. Successful therapists learn that the best way to help is to continually strive to be a better therapist—by reading, going to supervision, going to therapy themselves, looking at their issues, practicing being flexible, and adjusting their goals with their clients. If I measure myself by my clients' successes, I will go crazy. I will quit. And it's the same with parenting: if you measure yourself by your child's success, you may burn out too.

MOTIVATING WITH FEAR

Another way you might find yourself trying to exercise control is by making threats. I fall into that trap with my children. In particular, when my first child was a teenager, I thought my threats would prevent him from making some of the destructive choices that teenagers often make. I would often bring up my wilderness therapy program as a sort of cautionary device. I would make jokes about it—"If you do this thing, then you know you'll go away to the wilderness." Needless to say, this technique didn't work. After he eventually did go to the program, I learned he had always resented that threat and felt that the only way he could finally get rid of it was to go because the threat was so emotionally and intensely controlling. Though I didn't realize it at the time, by trying to threaten him *out* of it I ended up actually threatening him *into* it. Intimidating and controlling parenting undervalues our children's choices. It also uses up more parental energy and effort than just doing the necessary work of setting boundaries.

I have been amazed to see myself and other parents use intimidation to try to "scare" children into doing the right thing. This goes beyond informing the child about a consequence should they violate a certain rule or limit. It is an emotionally charged threat intended to frighten the child into following some rule so that the parent doesn't have to do the hard work of establishing and managing his own boundaries. Raising our voices, repeating the consequences, or amplifying the consequences are all ways we use fear to control our children. This behavior instead conveys the idea, "I am unhappy, and the key to my happiness is your changing. I will employ any means necessary toward that end." It is, ostensibly, telling your children "my happiness is your problem"—and it is the unhealthy seed of control-based parenting.

OUTCOME-BASED PARENTING

We teach our students in wilderness therapy the principle of "letting go of the outcome," meaning stop trying to manage the result. Sure, outcomes are important, but you don't need to be attached to them emotionally or spiritually. For parents, it doesn't mean that you don't adjust your approach based on your child's response. If I'm trying to communicate with or have an impact on someone, I will observe his or her response, *but I will not be tied to that response.*

Letting go of the outcome is a foundational principle of distinguishing between controlling and influencing people. So often with our children, the struggle to develop a sense of self and identity leads to resistance to any form of parental direction. Their internal dialogue tells them, "If I do what my parents want, I will lose my independence and sense of self." Even when our intentions are unspoken, what we don't say often leaks out through what we do say—and our children pick up on it. You can't cheat or hide your agenda as well as you think. Instead, state your intentions transparently and own them as yours.

An ultimate "letting go" moment occurred for me when I was working with a student on suicide watch. He said, "Yes, I'm suicidal, and right now I'm on suicide watch, but I'm going to wait to do it. It's going to be a nice day in one week or three weeks, and then you're going trust me. I'm going to be in a good mood,

The more covert your agenda, the more likely the child will find it threatening.

and you're going to think I'm doing better, and then I'm going to get off suicide watch. That's when I'm going to kill myself."

That scared the hell out of me. I told him, "Because you said that, you have earned the privilege to be on suicide watch for your entire stay at our program." But the fact of the matter is he was right. After he finished our program, of course he could eventually harm himself. We could keep him on suicide watch for two months, we could keep him in a locked facility for two years, but at some point he would have his opportunity. All I could do was be the best therapist I could be and then let go of the outcome. All I could do was offer a safe and secure and nurturing "container."

I can't force my daughter Olivia to eat her vegetables. What I can do is let her know that there is not going to be any other food served to her. That doesn't mean I am controlling her; it means I am being assertive with the boundaries and clear about my intentions. I am showing her how the world works and creating a miniature universe in my home to replicate the greater universe she will experience outside of it.

Whether or not the child learns such lessons is up to them. When a child says, "I'm not going to learn anything from this program," I'll reply, "Well, that says a lot more about you than it does about this program." There is an old saying I share with the kids: "The wise man learns more from the fool than the fool learns from the wise man." I have control over what I say and do, but what you think about me or how you respond to me is about you.

Sports offer wonderful illustrations of the relationship between our anxiety, our attempt to control the outcome, and our likelihood of reaching the target. Like a pitcher who learns to trust his throw or the tennis player who learns to trust her swing, our accuracy is actually impaired when we aim it too much. Self-trust is just as crucial in parenting. We learn to let go and trust ourselves as parents by focusing on our intentions, feelings, and objectives rather than obsessing over whether our actions will accomplish those objectives.

INFLUENTIAL PARENTING

Influential or assertive parenting is established through self-awareness. Everyone of us has room for improvement here. Sometimes that requires outside help, such as talking to a therapist. After all, it can be challenging to ask yourself, "What am I feeling? What's really going on? What are my intentions?" Be *honest* with yourself in order to get better at doing this. Exercise that "feeling muscle" by becoming aware of what you are trying to do.

Influential parenting is a virtue. It's brave and courageous. It takes a willingness to suffer and to go through pain. It's a balancing act. Ironically, it is the parents who are permissive that are the most controlling. It is important to show your child the connection between their behavior and the consequences of that behavior. The balance is creating structure and understanding whatever your child decides will provide him or her a valuable lesson.

Compare it to eating right. It's hard to maintain a balanced diet. Many tend to eat nothing for long periods of time and then eat a lot all at once, but really struggle with maintaining a balanced diet because being in the middle is the hardest place for many of us to be. An influential parent values autonomy while also providing structure. Your children will surely fail in some ways within these constraints, but a greater failure may often be prevented because of the boundaries you've established. Like I always say,

> *"I'll let my child slip down one or two stairs but*
> *I won't let him fall down a flight of stairs."*

It's the same with drugs, coming home late, or grades. These struggles are part of the process through which your children need to learn. I have let my children experiment with some of their own self-regulation with schoolwork rather than hovering over them and checking their grades online every day. At times, this self-direction model has led to failure. Find the balance between micromanaging and denial.

The only real service I can provide for my children and students is to outline the consequences so that they know how to prepare themselves for life. Like the proverbial leading the horse to water, all I can offer is my message.

Here is a simple example of how to do that. If you say to your six-year-old daughter, "Jane, if you eat your chicken and vegetables, then you can have a scoop of ice cream for dessert," then that's assertive parenting. That's presenting a logical consequence to an action. If you say to her, "One more bite! It's really good. Vegetables will make you strong. Come on, Jane, look at this chocolate ice cream. It's your favorite," then you are trying to control the child. Influential parenting accepts and trusts that whether the child follows the rules or not, the consequences and limits provided will allow him or her to learn a valuable lesson. You're managing the outcome by *selling* the ice cream. Better to just tell your child, "Here's the rule. Here's the consequence. Here's the reward. It's up to you." Do you want Jane to eat vegetables? Yes. Do you want your child to go to school and graduate? Yes. Do you want your child to use drugs? No. But attempting to modify behavior through use of emotional pressures— nagging, begging, pestering, lecturing, whining, scaring, etc.—is a form of control, and children naturally tend to rebel against that. Even young children can understand and tolerate consequences. What they cannot tolerate are manipulative attempts by parents to control them—at least not without developing unhealthy patterns and blurred boundaries in their lives.

GOOD PARENTING IS GOOD LIVING

Practice and exercise your feelings, and share your parenting goals with other adults and peers. Be ruthless and honest with yourself and others. It *does* take a village. I had a father once tell me he was worried about his child in the program and that he was at his limit. At the time he was serving a medical mission aiding underprivileged children, but felt powerless to help his own. "Brad, I have such a hard time being away," he told me. At that time, I had been missing my own child and I felt a spiritual connection with him. I said, "You know, here's what is happening. You're helping somebody out there. Somebody else is helping my child right now and I'm helping your child. We're all going to help each other and there's going to be balance. So reach out. Be interdependent. Be willing to ask for help. And know you're not the only one who feels this way."

Years ago during a weekly phone call with some parents, a father asked me, "If my child's problems are not my fault, then why do you spend so much time on our weekly phone calls talking about parenting?" I thought it was a fair question and had to think about it. And as I did, it came to me again:

> *Good parenting is its own reward. Good parenting is good living. It means being a better man, woman, person, friend, self, boss, or employee.*

Khalil Gibran's *The Prophet* reads, "Your children are not your children. Seek not to make them like you, but seek to be like them." Think of it this way: we get to participate in this thing called parenting and our difficult children are the gift that teaches us and invites us to find our best selves.

FEAR AND LOVE

Start from a place of love and faith rather than fear. Fear destroys creativity, blocks access to our emotional resources, and makes us hold on tighter to control. With the memory of hurt and grief aching in us, we try to ensure that we and our loved ones will not suffer pain. Yet we also know our pain gives us depth and helps us find our love and joy. There is no harder place to embrace this seeming contradiction than in the relationship with our children. To do so requires great strength. Our strength can come from believing in a higher power or from recognizing something greater than ourselves. It can come from letting go and trusting God, or the universe, or whatever it may be.

My son related a story from art school that describes how fear gets in our way. His teacher, observing him work on an oil-and-canvas piece, stopped and asked, "What are you doing? You seem to be tentative."

Jake responded, "I am scared. I like what I have done so far and don't want to ruin it."

"That is not how it works," the instructor said. "Your assignment has changed. I want you to keep painting until you ruin it. Be bold and daring. No one who has done anything fantastic has let the fear of failure ruin him. Great artists, athletes, and thinkers had to let go in order to achieve greatness. Fear ruins art. Fear restricts our creativity and for you to be a successful artist, you must dare to fail at it."

The same is true in our lives and in our relationships. Fear restricts our creativity and prevents access to our internal resources.

I often use *Star Wars* as a metaphor with my parents and students. In my work with children I avoid religious references, not just because families come from all different religious backgrounds but also because, in my experience, it is easy for children to associate religion with their parents and therefore want to reject it.

I ask them, "What's the fundamental difference between Darth Vader and Yoda?" Anakin, before he became Darth Vader, suffered a great loss: the death of his wife. And instead of letting this pain burn through him, he vowed never to suffer again. What was Vader's solution? Control. Darth Vader wanted domination. He wanted to control others. If someone didn't agree with him, then he killed that person. He operated from a place of fear.

Yoda, on the other hand, focused on self-mastery. He looked within himself to find peace, and he changed himself in order to achieve it.

What did Yoda do when he felt pain? He cried. When you look at all the major religions of the earth, you'll see that they all emphasize looking internally in order to master the self. They don't emphasize changing the actions of others, but rather changing your *reactions* to the way others behave.

Love is courageous and risky—and fear holds on tightly and doesn't let go. In order for us to grow, we must embrace our fears and travel the difficult road to knowing ourselves. We must be willing to feel.

Needing Your Child's Approval

I think there is a common theme among this current generation of parents that prevents them from effectively teaching children the lessons they want them to learn. It is a sort of hybrid, which I call "therapist-professor" parenting. I've noticed that many modern parents are drawn to a more "enlightened," almost professorial approach to parenting, as is illustrated in this humorous cartoon:

"DON'T YOU REALIZE, JASON, THAT WHEN YOU THROW FURNITURE OUT THE WINDOW AND TIE YOUR SISTER TO A TREE, YOU MAKE MOMMY AND DADDY VERY SAD?"

www.CartoonStock.com

We may laugh, but the joke highlights an important trap that many parents fall into. As parents and adults we are enticed by the idea of lecturing, sharing, and teaching, forgetting that this is not the way that young children often learn, change, and grow.

The sooner you let go of trying to get your kids to understand or agree, the sooner they are likely to "get it." It is almost as if they hold you hostage with their disagreement. Their "I don't get it" keeps you trapped in a cycle of debate. To that, I suggest the following response: "It's okay if you don't get it. You don't need to. But if you do *A*, then you will get *B*, and if you do *C*, then you will get *D*." This line of reasoning tends to eliminate the power struggle, which is not about rules or boundaries but thoughts and feelings.

Children can adjust to high levels of structure. I have seen them thrive within very strict structures. What they often cannot adjust to is the parent who tries to impose a belief, opinion, philosophy, or feeling onto his child.

My therapist, Dr. Jami Gill, shared a story that illustrates this maxim. Early in her career, Dr. Gill recommended Al-Anon to many of her patients whose loved ones engaged in addictive or destructive behaviors. She had heard many good things about the program from others, but had never attended the program herself. One day, while wandering into the cafeteria at the hospital where she worked, she interrupted an Al-Anon meeting. The members of the group welcomed her and invited her to stay, so she took the opportunity. She didn't participate, but she listened to what others shared. "I walked out of there with two lessons," she later said. "First, I am not responsible for my alcoholic husband. And second, you can't reason with a drunk." She was not married to an alcoholic herself, but the wisdom of this lesson can be generalized. Sometimes we are dumbfounded by our children's lack of rational thought. Young children seem to act, at times, with such a lack of insight, foresight, or logic that they can put a drunk to shame! We can reason with them until we are blue in the face, but the lessons won't take.

A few years ago, I watched my wife having a discussion with our three-year-old daughter, Olivia, about why she received a time-out for a tantrum. My wife spent several minutes explaining her reasoning for the time-out—but Olivia wasn't having it. Her responses were angry, irrational, and disrespectful toward my wife's clear explanation of the consequence.

After this lengthy exchange had finally ended, I asked my wife, "Why did you spend so much time explaining it to her instead of just giving her the time-out?" She said, "When I was young, I didn't feel heard or understood by my parents. We didn't talk about our feelings or problems. I want Olivia to feel like she has a say. I want to let her know that I am here to listen to her."

Though this way of thinking is admirable, it reduces Olivia to a projection rather than seeing her as the person she is. My wife was trying to repair her own childhood by giving our daughter what my wife may have lacked in hers. This mentality, despite its noble intentions, leaves Olivia out of the picture altogether. In this instance, her needs aren't seen at all. My wife was trying to get Olivia to feel a certain way—to feel like she is heard. This effort spent trying to get a child to feel a certain thing can oftentimes get in the way of the child's *actual* feelings.

As parents, we often try to control the outcome rather than simply expressing our message clearly. Then the child, in turn, attempts to hold us hostage by refusing to feel what we want them to feel unless we meet their demands. This dynamic might play out with your child thinking, "I will not feel what you want me to feel unless you do what I want you to do. I will calm down and go to bed as long as you come back in one minute." This power struggle is insidious because it is difficult to recognize. It leads us away from effective parenting and pushes us toward controlling and coercive parenting, even when we may have originally gone into the situation with the very best of intentions.

Early on in my experience as a wilderness therapist, I was often charged with delivering difficult news to my students. This was everything from telling students that they could not call home, to letting them know that their parents had not responded to a threatening letter, to informing them that they would be entering a long-term therapeutic boarding school—sometimes between twelve and thirty months. "Why?" they would often ask, seemingly wanting a cogent defense of the decision. Yet when I tried to explain the rationale behind the recommendations and decisions, my words left them unconvinced.

Finally, after explaining myself to one student on several occasions, only to have him return with more questions and counterpoints, I offered him a deal. I would give him a large bag of M&M's (the wilderness program diet is typically devoid of sugar or treats, so this was a significant prize) if he could tell me why *he* thought his parents and I recommended the follow-up program. In return he gave me a very clear and comprehensive explanation. He was able to thoughtfully articulate every reason we had considered in making the decision. Finally, he ended with "but I just don't like it." Our children have the information if we present it to them, so don't fall into the "Why?" trap. That question is merely an invitation for debate. Once we start debating, explaining, justifying, and defending our parenting, then we have lost the battle. There is an old saying that used to hang in our office:

> *"Arguing with a teenager is like wrestling with a pig in the mud. Sooner or later, you realize the pig likes it."*

While a child might not consciously enjoy the conflict, it does give them a sense of control. Worse, it ultimately exposes parental insecurities that can lead to a compromise of resolve.

Another aspect of wanting our children to "get it" is that if they do get it, then we will not be required to enforce our boundaries. Years ago, I dropped by the office of one of the therapists at our program. On the inside of his door, I observed a handwritten letter from a mother to her daughter. It read, "I hope you will grow up to be the kind of daughter that I will never have to say no to."

"That's crazy," I said, pointing to the letter.

"That's why I have it up there," he explained. "It's there to remind me and to remind parents that their children will always push back, even after weeks of success in our small, safe community."

Your children will learn more from who you *are*—from the way you carry yourself in the world—than what you say. The relationship you foster with yourself and them will create a pattern in the family that will teach more than any lecture ever could. They will remember your lectures—and they will give them to their children in turn. But what will have more impact will be the way you live. Tian Dayton says it so well:

> Our children don't become who we tell them to be, they become who we are. They live in their unspoken and sometimes unfelt emotional world. Much of parenting is implicit rather than explicit, which is why children become who we are rather than who we tell them to be. . . . Our children drink us up like little sponges. . . . Each moment we are parenting or, for that matter, living in front of our children, we are showing them who we want them to become. . . . The family is the family. . . . Tending to our relationships, our personal lives, and our bodies are all the right thing to do, not only for us, but for our kids.

Focus on how you live, how you work, how you make your way through the world, and how you interact with others. It is from the behavior you model that children learn the value and richness of a meaningful, intentional life.

THE JOURNEY OF THE HEROIC PARENT

WHAT IF I DO EVERYTHING RIGHT
AND IT STILL DOESN'T WORK?

Quite commonly, at the end of a presentation on communication and consequences, a parent will say, "But I think I have done all of this. I am not perfect, but I have done all of this, and none of it worked."

With empathy born out of dealing with my own daily stumbling in parenting, I will listen as they outline their efforts. So let's explore this question: What if you do everything "right" and it still doesn't work? There are a few elements that I would like you to consider first. It is critical to remember that it's not about you. Healthy parenting is its own reward. It creates a better life for you and your family. As I have said, being a healthy parent means being a better mother, father, brother, sister, and friend—a better *person*. This is the goal of healthy parenting: to be the best parent and human being that you can be. But the measure of that is in your own personal serenity, even when your children continue to struggle.

After my third child, Isabella, was born, my wife hardly ever put her down. By the time Bella was eight months old, Michelle hadn't been away from her for more than four hours at a time. As Bella approached nine months, Michelle's friends and I finally convinced her to take a four-day weekend and leave me to care for Bella and our two older children, aged eight and ten.

During the next four days, I was reminded how difficult the job of being a full-time caregiver can be. A low point came when, while changing Bella's diaper, I turned to grab a new diaper from the closet behind me and she fell three and a half feet to the hardwood floor. Everything happened in slow motion. She hit headfirst, and as I saw her neck bend, I thought I had paralyzed her. A cold wave washed over me. I immediately picked her up and held her gently. Her mouth was open wide and she was crying so hard that there was no sound escaping from her. With her cradled against me, I rushed to our neighbor's house to see if I should take her to the hospital or call an ambulance. The wise and experienced mother reassured me that babies are resilient and that she seemed to be okay since she was moving and crying. She suggested that I watch her closely, but assured me the baby would very likely be fine.

The morning after Michelle came back from what seemed like an eternity wrapped into four days, I got up to get dressed for work. I expected to be eager to return to work but something had changed. I felt a greater closeness to my children. A message echoed from a time eight years earlier, when my second child, Emma, had colic and could not be soothed. My professor comforted me, "She will be your greatest blessing." The morning I was set to return to work, I realized that we love our children not *in spite* of what we do for them, but *because* of what we do for them. Perhaps this is why, as my mother once observed, "We will love our children much more than we will love our parents."

As a parent, you do the work that you do for *yourself*. And you do it because you love your children and want them to be okay and to be happy. And if you do it well, then joy, love, and connection come back to you ten times over.

When my wife was having difficulty getting pregnant between our third and fourth children, we talked with a fertility doctor and also considered adoption. At the time, I was working with a very sweet set of older parents dealing with their adopted son, who was suffering from a fairly severe attachment disorder. He had also been diagnosed with bipolar disorder, and he often lashed out violently toward his parents. One day, during one of our weekly calls, we were discussing their sadness, fear, and grief as we revisited both the history with their son and his present course of treatment. We talked about one incident in particular, when their son threw a tantrum and threatened to kill his parents; he drew a picture of what the act would entail in front of many family members during a Thanksgiving gathering.

At the end of the call, I mentioned that my wife and I were considering adoption, but that stories like these from families who adopt children who have attachment disorder caused me great concern. I asked these parents, "If you knew everything you knew now about how life was going to be with your son before you adopted him, would you still do it?" Immediately and without wavering, they both shared that they never had a second thought. It was a real trial, to be sure, but they had no regrets about the decision to take this baby into their lives and to raise him. This story illustrates, again, that parenting is its own reward.

I think the next issue related to doing things "right" is about our anger, resentment, and expectations. Last year, I was talking with a friend and colleague, who, like me, had sent his son away for treatment. Reaching this point had been just as significant for him as it had been for his son. He had lost weight, started practicing yoga, and quit drinking; although no one considered him a problem drinker, he saw it as a sign of solidarity and support for his son. His son returned home after two months in a program, and my friend had called me to share some of his frustrations. He was angry because his son had relapsed. He had caught him smoking pot, which was one of the reasons he was sent away to treatment in the first place. The father talked about how he had not had a drink since his son had started the intervention, yet now his son was using again.

I asked for permission to give an observation. He welcomed it. "A few months ago, when you told me you had stopped drinking, I was suspicious," I told him. "I have seen many parents make changes in their lives—some go so far as to move their whole family to create a new start for a child after an intervention—because they think that it will be the key to changing their child. Some go to great lengths and make huge sacrifices. When you told me about all the changes you had made 'for yourself,' I suspected that you might be doing it for your son. Your anger may be evidence that you were, in fact, doing these things for him with the expectation that if you did everything right, then your son would owe you or be obligated to you or simply see you as an inspiration and then want to stay clean and sober." My friend, a very talented parent educator himself, was surprised to find that this was true. He shared that although he taught this very principle to parents all the time, he had fooled himself into believing he had made all these changes for himself. Until this moment, he hadn't realized he was doing these things with a powerful expectation attached.

After watching a webinar of one of my parent lectures about control vs. influence, my wife told me that a question a parent asked at the end of the broadcast had resonated with her: "What if consequences don't work?" She shared with me how she feels the most anger when she "does everything right," and Olivia, our then-four-year-old, still doesn't do what she is supposed to do. Getting Olivia to bed is a big issue, for example. Michelle has read two books on how to get a child to go to bed and sleep through the night. She follows all the steps. But nothing has helped.

Part of the problem—or the solution, depending on how you look at it—is how we measure success as parents. When a parent says, "But I did all of this. I am not perfect, but I was a pretty good parent." My response is, "Congratulations. You must have a great deal of peace. Serenity and peace are the result of healthy parenting, not well-behaved children. The question you have about getting it right suggests that doing it right causes someone else to change. I am sure you were great. And your child's struggles are not about you. Their struggles are their own."

As long as you keep requiring your child to agree with you and say that you're a good parent, then you are asking them to be responsible for your self-esteem. No child needs that. It's a heavy burden to carry around your parent's self-worth. All of us are willing to make great sacrifices in order to take care of our parents, but this process infects our relationships with others and leads us away from good self-care and into maladaptive ways of coping. It is up to you to find your measure for your success somewhere else.

Removing the burden of your ego from your child is one of the greatest gifts you can give as a parent.

But this is difficult because this is how we were parented. We were taught, most of us, that our success and failures were a reflection of our parents.

Recently I was visiting the office of a friend and therapist in the Los Angeles area. He works mostly with young adults who are suffering from addiction and their families. On his wall I saw a photo of John Belushi sitting on the floor of the *Saturday Night Live* studio. "Why do you have this?" I asked him.

"I love that photo," he replied. "I use it all the time in working with families. The television network and the family hired a bodyguard to watch out for John, but he still died of a drug overdose in that body-guard's arms. This story can be terrifying for families to hear, but it serves to illustrate our powerlessness over others."

An adult friend recently took what she thought was advice from me. I say "thought" because I actually did not suggest anything specific; I simply supported her in her exploration of healthy boundaries. After a wonderful weekend with her mother, she decided to broach the subject of her childhood in the car on the way to dinner. My friend started to talk about some things she was exploring in therapy, and how she had come to realize that as a child she didn't feel safe to speak her feelings in the family. Immediately, her mother interrupted, "Oh, so we are going to talk about what a horrible mother I was. I was a single mother and your father was gone and I did the best I could do." Her mother went on, clearly upset, "Just pull over and let me out of the car right here." My friend backpedaled and apologized to her mother, soothing her mother's obvious fear and guilt, realizing that she still wasn't safe with her mother.

When my friend reported back the discussion to me, she started with, "Great idea that was! Thanks! I tried to start a discussion with my mom about how I didn't feel heard as a child and she freaked out. That didn't work!"

"Work?" I asked. "What was your goal? If your goal was to change your mom, then you may have misunderstood our discussion. Parents are crazy," I kidded. "I supported you in finding your voice with your mother and stating your truth. I never suggested it would have any particular desired effect on her."

The principle we return to with this story and with our children is that assertive, intentional, and empowered parenting only guarantees that we are healthy. It does not promise to "work" in changing anyone else but us. When we use it hoping to change another, we are not expressing ourselves honestly and assertively.

The question of "What if I do it all right and it doesn't work?" is flawed in and of itself. The question assumes that because you do your job as a parent that your children will respond. The question removes the child's agency. And it is in reconsidering the question that we find the answer. "It" works when you are happy, clear, and less anxious. The only outcome that can be guaranteed from healthy communication and clear boundaries is that you will live a happier life.

CHAPTER SEVEN

PARENTAL GUILT, SHAME, AND OUR CHILDREN

Guilt can undermine our confidence and erode our connection with our children, preventing us from allowing them to experience what they need to in order to stretch and grow.

THIS CHAPTER FOCUSES ON THE RELATIONSHIP BETWEEN our children and our guilt. Liberating yourself from guilt and anxiety will not only offer you relief but will increase your ability to parent effectively. But to examine the effects of guilt and shame in our lives, we will first need to make a critical distinction between guilt and moral conscience.

Why does my child blame me for their problems? Parents express anger, disappointment, frustration, and even rage at the blame their children place on them. The mistake of applying cause-and-effect logic to parenting when our children struggle is one way we might teach them to blame us.

The Shame Cycle—which illustrates patterns of shame in our lives and the lives of our children—is detailed in this chapter. I will propose an alternative as well as present a set of skills that can help us steer clear of shame and its deleterious effects on us and on our children.

GUILT VS. SHAME

There's a common notion that guilt is feeling badly about something that you did, while shame is feeling badly about yourself fundamentally.

Perhaps the two words might describe a level or a degree of feeling, and shame being the more intense of the two, but essentially they effect people in similar ways. In her now-famous TED Talk on vulnerability, Brené Brown attempts to make a distinction:

> Shame is a focus on self; guilt is a focus on behavior. Shame is "I am bad." Guilt is "I did something bad." How many of you, if you did something that was hurtful to me, would be willing to say, "I'm sorry. I made a mistake"?

The entire audience raised their hands in agreement. Yet in my work with couples and families, I don't see this playing out in people's lives. I don't know many people who find it easy to get past their guilt and admit they did something wrong and apologize. I am not exactly sure what guilt is, if not some form of shame. If guilt is a less intense version of shame, it is my experience as a husband, father, and therapist that people struggle to admit to mistakes or hurting others. Perhaps there is a link here between guilt and shame. Perhaps shame-based personalities do equate what they do with who they are. And because hurting someone is not okay—"you shouldn't be that way"—the distinction between guilt and shame is meaningless.

I want to challenge the idea of "healthy" guilt and shame. It is my belief that shame is one of the most destructive elements in the psyche. It's rare when I'm treating somebody presenting with guilt or shame—

even if it's discussed in terms of behavior change—that I see shame translate into change over the long run. Shame is either transitory or so internalized that it actually leads people to hide parts of the self and create new defense mechanisms.

That is precisely the thing that I think is most destructive about shame. If the distinction between guilt and shame is just a matter of degree, then we should talk about the level of shame. Shame tells us that we are unacceptable, repulsive, or deserve rejection. The concept of healthy guilt is akin to saying that there can be healthy poison or humane cruelty. Guilt- or shame-based behavior negatively affects our emotional and spiritual life because it blocks us from achieving self-awareness. From the story in Genesis, after Adam and Eve transgressed by eating from the tree of knowledge of good and evil, they hid themselves from God:

> And the eyes of them both were opened, and they knew that they were naked;
> and they sewed fig leaves together, and made themselves aprons. And they heard the voice of the Lord God walking in the garden in the cool of the day: and Adam and his wife hid themselves from the presence of the Lord God amongst the trees of the garden.
> And the Lord God called unto Adam, and said unto him, "Where art thou?"
> And he said, "I heard thy voice in the garden, and I was afraid, because I was naked; and I hid myself."
> And He said, "Who told thee that thou wast naked?"

Shame and guilt are the forces that cause us to retreat from others, from help and from needed support. We hide our humanness in the recesses of our unspoken selves, beyond the healing power of community. Exposing our whole selves to the light means a willingness to talk about and acknowledge it and we need a safe context for that—a context where people won't recoil or shun. In attending therapy or a parent group, we can find people who accept us *and* our imperfections. An alcoholic walks into an AA meeting to expose his dirty secrets, and an old-timer says to him, "You're welcome here. Sit next to me." That grace offers us the courage to look more honestly at ourselves. And with compassion from others, we can heal and learn to live a more healthy life.

Using judgment, guilt, and shame to try to manage our children's behavior may work in the short term, but it creates a structure in the personality that prevents whole and healthy development. When we feel ashamed we want to shrink, we want to disappear. We deny, we resist, we repress. The great danger in shame and guilt is that they actually impede change because they prevent us from looking at the most difficult sides of ourselves and from exploring and working on those parts. Shame can also block our sense of right and wrong.

Self-awareness is an ideal and striving for that ideal is a key message in this book. In order for us to be more aware, we have to go past the sentinels of shame that stand guard and tell us that we "should" or "ought not" to be, feel, think, or behave a certain way. Moving past shame, we can learn to experience and express compassion toward ourselves. It is only this kind of self-love that will allow us to truly heal and parent from a place of clarity.

The antidote to shame is grace. When we experience a feeling of nonjudgment from another person, our shame cannot survive. This is why people seek therapy or support groups, or forgiveness from a higher power. Through acknowledging one's shame and seeking forgiveness, they are more able to do the honest work of improving their lives.

WHERE DOES SHAME COME FROM?

We use guilt and shame in parenting because that is how we were raised by our own parents. We were taught that our behaviors, needs, and mistakes upset our parents. We were taught that we were responsible for these feelings in them and that we needed to change or get in line to avoid upsetting Mom or Dad.

I sat in a group during an "impact letter" reading some time ago. A sixteen-year-old girl was reading her letter, where her parents described the reasons for enrolling her in our program. In the letter, the parents, and in this case the grandfather too, related the details of her story. The young woman read to the group, through her tears, accounts of heroin addiction, stealing, prostitution, and acts of aggression toward her family. As she finished, the group sat patiently for a few moments. The group was silent but for the sound of her sobs. Finally, someone asked, "What are you feeling?"

She responded, "I feel so bad for what I put my parents through."

This is one of the most common reactions our students share after reading the impact letter, but this time I was especially incredulous. "You just read a letter about a potentially fatal level of drug use, prostitution, and many other self-destructive behaviors. And your first reaction was how you hurt your parents. I don't think that is the point of this letter and I know it is not the point of this program. The purpose is understanding how you are hurting *yourself,*" I told her.

Yet this reaction was hardwired into her—and it's the same with many of us. We make reference to others' feelings in deciding whether we are doing the right or wrong thing. But when we parent our children in this way, we create a dynamic in which our sons and daughters are always seeking approval—and thus more susceptible to peer pressure.

The young woman who believes she is responsible for her mother's feelings will also feel she is responsible when her friends are upset that she doesn't want to go to a party where there is alcohol.

Shame starts early. When a baby sees his mother exhausted from having to change another dirty diaper, he interprets this as "I am bad for causing her frustration." You may think I'm exaggerating, but think of how we refer to certain newborns as "good" babies, meaning babies that are quiet or happy or peaceful—not temperamental, reactive, or colicky.

Later, these messages become more overt as parents (and others) tell children "to be less needy," or to "not be so sensitive." Instead of finding the strength to explore and make sense of the need or sensitivity, we make the child feel "wrong." When people don't want to own their own sense of failure in responding to another's needs, they project those "bad" feelings onto the other by suggesting the feeling was caused by him.

As adults, this process might not seem rational to us, but this is what happens in a child who does not have the capacity to rationalize and separate their behaviors from who they are as a person. When this happens to us as children, we carry that same reaction into adulthood. Then when our children get upset with us, it triggers that old reaction: we feel a sense of shame and think, "I did something, and I'm responsible for that, so I'm bad." This is why shame and guilt impede parenting.

This is the origin of the struggle we have with our boundaries and our sense of what is "right." We have difficultly in applying self-care, believing it to be selfish. But the repression of healthy self-care will be expressed in some unconscious way. Often this takes the form of parents needing children to provide them with unconditional love. But this can never satisfy us because the injury occurred in our past, and it is there that it must be addressed.

One of the most insidious aspects of shame is that it works temporarily. When I am lazy or not centered, I use it to try to control my children or my spouse. I might try to disguise that shame in the form of a question, such as saying, "Really? That's what you were thinking when you made that ridiculous decision?" But you know and I know that's not really a question; it's a statement. It's me stating, "I want you to feel so ashamed and embarrassed that you don't do this again." Shaming is one of the most tempting and damaging things we can do in our relationships. "You ought to be ashamed of yourself," we tell children. There are better ways to communicate that don't come with so many negative side effects.

WHERE ELSE CAN WE LOOK TO FIND OUR MORAL BEARINGS?

Perhaps the greatest problem with the concepts of guilt and shame is the notion that they are connected to our conscience, that they help us determine "right" and "wrong." Guilt *can* be in line with our sense of morality at times, but it is just as often not the case, and can lead us to do harmful things to our loved ones and ourselves. The young woman who feels badly for not having sex with her boyfriend may feel guilt, but this does not distinguish between right and wrong. She perceives the wrongness inside of her when her behaviors hurt another. Feelings of guilt and shame are simply an indication of our belief that our behavior will be perceived by another as hurtful, leading to potential rejection from that person.

When I ask parents why they avoid doing what's best for their child, the most common response is "I feel guilty." But it can be important to consider that shame and guilt often lead us to make the worst decisions in our lives and in our parenting.

As parents, we need to tolerate guilt in order to do the right thing for our children.

Part of what will help you in learning to tolerate guilt is recognizing the origin of guilt and shame in your own childhood and reminding yourself that those feelings are different than and separate from your conscience or moral compass. Seeing this more clearly, you will begin to change the way you parent, and you will develop healthier patterns in all of your relationships.

If guilt and shame are not reliable sources of right and wrong, then where *do* we find our morality? I propose that it comes from love. A healthy love for ourselves and an empathic connection to others are both powerful sources of morality. Empathy is developed as we become more aware of our whole selves—our thoughts, feelings, and the hidden parts that were left behind long ago. Discovering who we truly are must involve an exploration of our childhood. It is part of the hero's journey. And when we become more clear about who we are and why we are this way, we will develop a clearer idea of others—most importantly our children. When we truly know ourselves and our children, we can see past their surface reactions to their deeper needs. There are no detours or negative side effects when love is our source of morality. Where guilt and shame build barriers, love tears them down.

Much of my work as a therapist and a parent educator is helping people to understand and love themselves. If they can love, forgive, and make peace with themselves, then they can move forward with a clear conscience. Love beckons while shame repels. The higher law of love causes us to feel pain, sadness, and empathy—and those emotions are far more effective at changing a negative behavior than shame.

Love must exist for *oneself* in order for it to exist toward others. In working with sex offenders, I learned how this works. The first thing that most people would say about sex offenders is that they lack empathy for others. This accurate assumption is at the core of their problem. So do we simply tell the offenders stories of how they hurt their victims? No, that approach has been shown to be ineffective. Many of the offenders I worked with endured some form of acute or chronic abuse themselves. To survive that abuse, they learned to *not feel*. They turned themselves into an object because they were being treated like one, and because objects don't feel pain. Since we tend to assume sameness among ourselves, it's difficult to imagine others being fundamentally different. So these offenders viewed others as objects too—*objects without feeling*. Therefore, in their minds they were not hurting another person, but merely acting on an object.

The way to help someone feel empathy and connection is to teach and allow them to feel *their pain*.

This is how we parent with love rather than shame. We teach our children to feel—to feel *everything*, not just what we want them to feel. And we tolerate their feelings by sitting with them and letting them feel.

The natural extension of that process is that they will be able to connect to other people who hurt.

When someone learns to feel their feelings, they can recognize it in others. This is how we develop empathy.

PARENTAL GUILT

Many parents don't allow themselves the space to set healthy boundaries, or they don't require accountability because they are handcuffed by guilt. This guilt could be about mistakes they make, or things that they (or others) do that cause the child pain. In the case of an adopted child, the adoptive parents may feel "bad" for the child and his previous circumstances and try to make it up to him by indulging the child. A divorced parent might struggle to be assertive with her child because she perceives the pain of the divorce as the cause of the child's behavior. When you look at yourself clearly and responsibly, when you try to be a good parent and don't indulge in feeling guilty for your mistakes, then you give your child's life and choices back over to them, and they will feel more powerful. They will have a greater sense of efficacy, and will learn from their mistakes rather than blaming those mistakes on you.

The expression of guilt usually sounds like, "I feel bad for hurting him." Guilt suggests, "If I hurt or upset someone else, I have done the wrong thing." But the problem with that kind of thinking is it leaves parents rudderless. They compromise boundaries and doubt themselves because they are taking direction from the child and his protestations.

Unfortunately, more often than opening us up to compassion and change, guilt triggers defensiveness. In examining your guilt, ask yourself these questions: Is the guilt productive? Does it motivate you? Does it lead you to thinking about what you plan to do? If the guilt is productive, then the anxious feelings will disappear quite quickly. It will motivate you, and you'll move forward from it. Lingering guilt, however, is almost never healthy.

It is remarkable how often guilt and shame prevent rather than encourage parents (and children) to do the "right" thing. Guilt makes us pay too much attention to how others feel about us, rather than focusing on what is the best course of action for ourselves. I encourage parents to "feel the guilt, and do the 'right' thing anyway." We are not responsible for what others think about us, including our children. We're responsible for our own actions, for being good parents, and for being good people. In turn, our children are responsible for the way that they choose to respond. Don't engage in the cycle of dependence. Let them feel or think about you how they want. It's not about your kids loving you or not; it's about you loving them. And loving them means you sometimes have to do difficult things, even things that might make them hate you.

CAUSE-AND-EFFECT PARENTING TEACHES BLAME

There are two principles in family therapy that address the limitations of cause-and-effect thinking in families. These concepts are *equifinality* and *equipotentiality*. The former allows that different ends can come from the same beginning, and the latter that different beginnings can lead to the same end.

Imagine two individuals who both end up working with abused children. One comes from an abusive family, and one comes from a nurturing family. Despite their diverse backgrounds, they end up in the same place. This can happen in your family. You may have one child who ends up addicted to drugs, committing crimes, struggling with mood disorders, or lacking empathy while another child is successful, empathic, hardworking, and responsible. The ideas of equifinality and equipotentiality again serve to remind us that we cannot control every outcome.

Measuring one's success by one's own behaviors and not by the reactions of one's children is central to effective parenting. If we ask ourselves, "How will I know if I have done the right thing in my parenting?" the answer cannot come from the successes or failures of our children. This reduces them to objects and removes their responsibility from the equation.

Immanuel Kant wrote, "Act in such a way that you treat humanity, whether in your own person or in the person of any other, never merely as a means to an end, but always at the same time as an end." In other words, do the right thing strictly because it's the right thing. Make a decision for your family and your child because it feels good and healthy.

Healthy parenting is the end, not the means to an end. My job as a therapist is to teach you how to become a healthy parent, not how to raise healthy kids. In fact, sometimes the relationship between being a healthy parent and raising healthy kids is almost coincidental. I want to be clear about that. You can be the best parent who ever lived and you can still have a child who ends up doing horrible things, living an unhappy life, and being very angry with you. Alternately, you can be a bad parent and have a child that transcends it all to become a wonderful, compassionate person. Parenting skills and principles don't change children; they change parents. And that change in a parent can have a wonderful impact on a child.

I once taught a parent meeting in which a woman was explaining her grandchild's background and why he was in the program. She described how the young man's father had left by the time he was two years old and that they boy never saw him again. And how, at age eight, the boy awoke one morning to find his mother dead in her bed after she had battled obesity for many years. After that, the boy had moved in with his grandparents. A year later, the boy's grandfather, with whom he was very close, died. The following year, as the child was walking through a crosswalk he was hit by a car, leaving him permanently scarred and partially crippled. After outlining the litany of painful experiences suffered by her grandchild, she turned to the parents sitting next to her, "That is why my grandson is here. Why is your son here?"

I gently interrupted, "That's not why he is here. Although those wounds need to be addressed and healed, he is here because he has developed a rage problem and he's a drug addict. He's not here simply because of something that happened to him, he's here because of how he chooses to respond to what happened to him." Despite my sympathy for the boy and the many tragedies in his life he had endured, I had to make it clear to everyone that we are not defined by our past experiences.

Our children sense that we have a stake in their successes or failures—often too much of a stake. This sense of being smothered can be described as psychologically swallowing them up so that they become part of us. And while the style is often described in pop culture as "overly identified," it is essentially abandonment because this fusion of selves does not see or acknowledge the "other." After a parent group in which I had mentioned my son's acceptance to a prestigious art school, someone approached me and offered congratulations. I was confused. After all, it was not my success. In fact, I think his accomplishment was in spite of rather than because of me. But we often think of our children as extensions of ourselves due to the way we were taught to define the parent-child relationship.

One of the most important contributions we can make to our child's self-esteem is the ability to forgive ourselves. When you do, you can courageously hold your child accountable for their actions. This is not an abdication of your responsibility as a parent, but rather a refocusing. In the book *The Anatomy of Peace*, parents attend an initial seminar as their children embark on a wilderness therapy intervention. As they conclude the first day of parent education, two parents reflect on their day.

"I'm a bad mom."

"I think you're being too hard on yourself," Lou said. "The truth is Cory has been a terribly difficult boy. It's not your fault."

"It depends what you mean by that, Lou," she said, regaining her composure. "I understand that I may not be responsible for the things he's done. But I am responsible for what I've done."

ACCOUNTABILITY

When we learn to shed the shackles of guilt and stop trying to defend ourselves, we allow our children to be responsible for themselves. When burdened with guilt, we have difficulty requiring anything of them because, after all, they have the perfect excuse: a fallible parent to blame. Part of our job is to be empathetic toward our children, but another part of our job is to hold them accountable for their own actions. They must make their own choices and determine what their attitude will be as they go through life.

What makes accountability different from blame? Accountability recognizes the effect of your behavior on others, but you do not assume blame for that effect. Accountability sees the impact you have, but does not overwhelm you with the effect of that impact. Accountability is courageous and honest; it shows itself in the light. Unlike guilt and shame, it does not shrink or hide under inspection. Accountability looks you right in the eye and does not drop its chin to avoid shameful feelings. Accountability apologizes for itself—but not too much. It does not promise change strictly to ease its own sense of responsibility.

Admitting accountability means that you recognize ownership of a particular situation. Accountability is a willingness to pay for what you did, but without getting to decide the terms. When I worked with sex offenders for the state of Utah, a lot of them wanted to write apology letters to their victims. I would say, "I don't know if your victim is ready for that. I don't know that forgiveness gets to come on your terms. In fact, I think that it's probably still your ego that wants to write that letter now. You need to wait for your victim to be ready to forgive. You cannot force them."

When my son wrote a "letter of accountability" during his wilderness stay, he stated, "I hope you won't use this letter against me." My response to him was, "I will use it any way that I want to. This is *my* accountability letter. And if you really are accountable, then you'll understand that I might be upset, I might be angry, and I may or may not talk to some of your friends' parents about it." Pure accountability asks nothing in return from the other. A person who's accountable doesn't try to cut a deal and say, "Will you grant me immunity or less punishment if I do this thing?" The accountable person will say, "I will do whatever it takes to make this right, and if you don't forgive me today, tomorrow, or the next day, then I can deal with that. I can pay that price."

THE SHAME CYCLE

I first developed this model after observing children in wilderness therapy who experienced great shame about their past behaviors. It was hard for them to hear their parents describe the behaviors and the impact they had on the family. Sometimes the child would reach tears, or sometimes the child would put up a wall of indifference, but both responses indicate a sense of shame and guilt. "I never really knew how much this affected my parents," a child might say. Or, "I realize how much they love me. I now see the consequences of my mistakes." On the surface these statements might be appealing. Many parents are soothed by such a response, although some are suspicious because they have heard words like this in the past—without any change in behavior.

When I first started working with children in a therapy program, I was impressed by the strong reactions that guilt seemed to evoke in people. I saw how parents employed guilt with their children, and how it seemed to motivate the kids to agree to change. But eventually I saw many children revert to the same or even worse behaviors. I learned there are more sustainable motivators than guilt. Now I'll tell the students, "Guilt can be the ignition switch that can turn on change, but you don't keep cranking the key once the engine is already started. If you do, then you're going to ruin the starter, and the car is no longer going to work." Unfortunately, some people continue turning the key of guilt on themselves or others.

I've seen children become despondent and hopeless, which makes it difficult for them to face their mistakes and move forward without paralyzing anxiety about every potential future mistake.

Children will make mistakes every day, every week, and every year—and some of those mistakes are going to look similar to their old patterns.

If a child carries too much shame, it becomes too painful to face his or her past mistakes. In these cases, I tell the child, "I hear you. I hear that you feel horrible, and that's fine. I'm not going to tell you what to feel. But in order to make a positive change, you can't let yourself be overcome by shame and how your past actions made others feel. Otherwise you will never be able to move away from those actions." Then I start questioning them to encourage a positive shift. "What are you going to do to make your life better?" I might ask. "Because yes, you hurt your loved ones. You affected them, because they care about you and they were injured by your behavior. But you're going to get mad at them someday. In fact, you're going to get mad at them often, because that's what happens when you're in a close relationship with someone. Guilt is anger turned inward. Buddha said, 'Hatred does not cease by hatred, but only by love; this is the eternal rule.' Your motivation has to be doing good for its own sake in order to be healthy. Doing work for others is not sustainable. Sure, your parents are angry with you now, but their anger is not your burden. If you want to move on and create a healthy new beginning, it is important to move through shame. They too will benefit from letting go of their anger."

What is this cycle that kids go through? How can a child seem to be doing fine one moment, then struggling the next? When I tell a parent their son or daughter is struggling with shame, they have a hard time talking about it or relating to it. It often doesn't make sense to them. I created this model to illustrate the cycle and offer an exit strategy out of our shame.

Stages 1 and 2: Perception. Perhaps the most important part of this cycle occurs when—and only when—the individual has the capacity to read the wants and needs of someone else. While this capacity may not be synonymous with empathy, the child who struggles with shame does have a perceptive ability and sensitivity to others. This is a necessary ingredient in what parents call the "manipulative" child. Shame can begin at a very basic level. For a child, it can be as simple as,

"When I get hurt, my mom cries. When I have an accident instead of making it to the toilet, my dad yells." The child internalizes the reactions to those behaviors, feels bad about them, and attempts to repress them. Parents often reward these reactions since it seems to demonstrate empathy on the kid's part. A mother might think, "Oh, my child saw that I was sad, and now she is no longer doing the thing that made me sad, so she is kind, smart, and empathetic." Most of this is subconscious, of course, not consciously manipulative. However, problems begin when the child focuses on the needs of others and ignores her own. The child then begins to confuse her own happiness with the happiness of others. "If I don't have an accident, or if my parents don't see me have an accident, then my parents will be happy."

Stage 3: Repression. The next process is triggered because the child cannot attend to both his own needs and the needs of the other at the same time. The two ideas begin competing with one another. "I can't express myself. I can't come home from school upset. I can't share that with my family and get them upset, because that will be bad." So the child stops expressing, talking, feeling, or taking care of himself in some crucial way.

Stage 4: Self-Care. Although the child receives reinforcement for attending to the needs of others, this starves him of his own essential needs and desires. The child wants to get his needs met somehow, so he finds maladaptive ways to meet them. He tries cutting himself, drinks a lot, uses drugs, and overeats. But, of course, these are all counterfeit ways of meeting needs. They're replacements. And they don't work because they're not *really* fulfilling. Attempts to get a need met in unhealthy or maladaptive ways are called symptoms; patterns of symptoms are referred to as diagnoses. Parents often ask me, "Who will my child be with in your program? Hopefully not drug addicts," or kids with another issue. But the issues are all really the same. While the medicators may look different, mental health and addiction issues are a child's best attempt to meet a core need or address an underlying struggle. Often this is the overwhelming shame they carry. I hope that in understanding this principle both parents and children can remove some of the shame of the various types of suffering that afflict our children.

Perhaps the greatest danger at this stage is that certain medicators can be very addictive. Instead of having symptoms, the symptoms have you. Alcohol or gambling may initially serve to offer the individual an escape, but after an addiction develops it actually creates more problems, and the addict is unable to think her way out of it without a great deal of support. Because the core dynamics are deeply internalized, the exit might take some very painful and long-term work in therapy or recovery.

Stage 5: Performing for the Other. The child experiences "pleasing others" as a mandate rather than a choice. This explains why many parents will remark, "He thinks we need him to be perfect, or be a star athlete, or be this or that, but we really just want him to be happy." Of course the child complains that his parents will really only be happy if he is this or that. In a certain way, both child and parent are right. "When I get good grades, it makes my mom happy, so I'll get good grades for her. When I play soccer, I can see that my dad is proud, so I'll play soccer to make him proud." In working with parents, I see many of them confused when this pattern is revealed. A father might say, "I never asked him to play soccer. I just wanted him to be happy. Sure, when he started playing I was happy, but that's because I thought he was happy. He didn't need to play soccer for me." But that's the experience of the child in the cycle. And then he moves on to the next phase, in which he believes he's being forced to sacrifice himself and his own needs for others, and the resentment builds. He starts to alienate himself from others and blames them for not allowing him to meet his own needs. He is still trying to make others happy, but regardless of how hard he tries he can't make himself happy, so the maladaptive or symptomatic behavior increases, and the resentment for being "forced" builds.

Stages 6 and 7: Buildup and Blow-up. Finally, in many cases, there's a blow-up or face-to-face confrontation. This can be literal or metaphorical. The metaphor is the violation and rejection of any or all of the parents' values and rules. The child might be caught with drugs or having promiscuous sex. Behavior also can be directed inward, such as in the case of self-harm, but this injury is an expression of anger at part of the self. Instead of tolerating the anxiety that comes with that and looking at the deeper issues that trigger these behaviors, the child might blame you. "I hate you because you have caused so many problems for me," he might say. He tries to deny everything he believes in and has learned because he would rather deal with that blow-up than the anxiety that comes from failing to make you, his parent, happy. At that point, you might find it hard to understand that your child is acting this way out of shame.

When a parent describes an incident from this stage, they often follow it with, "I just wish he had more shame." But it's the opposite problem: he has too much shame.

Instead, he is sacrificing his own needs in order to make others happy, and it's gotten to the point where it so negatively affects his life that he doesn't know how to carry on. This is how powerful shame can become.

Stage 8: Regret. Then, through an intervention, a letter, or getting caught, the child feels guilty. The inflated self-image they experienced is deflated, and they feel horrible. Not grounded, not humble, but deflated. They feel like nothing, and want to disappear. They're horrible children. This is the "honeymoon" phase. And that's the danger of this cycle: it can go around and around, and after the guilt you fall back into the pattern of trying to please others. Indeed, there is often a tendency to return to pleasing behaviors to sooth the sting of guilt that comes as they "realize" how they have hurt others. Alternatively, they may shut out all feeling, developing apathy toward others. This provides relief and is the seed of antisocial (lacking empathy) personality traits.

HOW DO WE GET OUT?

The only way out of the cycle is through the door of guilt. We have to learn to tolerate our painful feelings of shame. Harriet Lerner illustrates this in *The Dance of Anger* with the story of an adult woman trying to set a healthy boundary with her father: "No matter how long I'm in therapy, I still feel guilty if I say no to my father. But if I keep saying yes, I'm going to feel angry. So, if I'm going to change, I guess I will just have to learn to live with some guilt for a while."

Discovering the origin or source of our guilt and shame can help make it tolerable. We can learn where our shame comes from and explore and challenge it in its original context by literally or metaphorically speaking to the voices. As we've seen, those origins are often deep in our psyches because they began early in our childhoods, and were learned long before we had words or complex thoughts. Therefore, they are coded in those parts of the brain that are emotional rather than rational, logical, and verbal. But they are still there, and we have to face them in order to overcome them. These are the dragons Campbell identifies: personal ghosts with whom we must do battle in order to find our mountaintops.

You want your children to learn to function without you, to be able to navigate the world in a healthy and moral way. But this only becomes possible as they differentiate action and emotion and learn how to think, feel, and act for themselves. In our wilderness program, I have told children many times, "I don't want you to change for me. I don't want you to do it for your parents. I want you to do it because it benefits *your* life."

My therapist has a poster hanging in her office entitled "Words of Higher Enlightenment." It addresses all those things that we don't like to see in ourselves: giving up, failing, flopping, surrendering, breaking down, and more.

WORDS
Drop Out, Fail, Quit, Lose, Relax, Give In, Flunk, Let Go, Empty, SURRENDER, Wait, Give Over, Mellow Out, Slow Down, Don't, Forget, Submit, Fade Away, Relinquish, Withdraw, Flop, Give Up, Chill, Yield, Back Out, Forgo, Resign, Acquiesce. Sink. Escape, Fizzle, Capitulate, Flag, Droop, Release, Drop The Ball, Defer, Sacrifice, Wash Out, Miss, Poop Out, Bend, Moderate, Rest, Stumble, Tame, Weaken, Calm, Teeter, Botch, Break Down, Lay An Egg, Flounder, Drag, Crap Out, Rest, Give Out, Ease Up, SURRENDER, Slow Down, Soften, Collapse, Let Up, Modulate, Diminish, Cushion, Offset, Give Over, Gentle, Renounce, *of* Abandon, Leave.
HIGHER ENLIGHTENMENT

Gill, Jami, D. *Finding Human,* North Charleston, SC: Create Space, 2014.

The idea is that we are enlightened only when we are willing to see these things in ourselves. Mahatma Gandhi taught, "The only devils in this world are those running around in our own hearts, and that is where all our battles should be fought." As depicted in the eponymous movie based on his life, he responded to a question about how he had fared in that battle, and confessed that he had not been a good warrior: "That's why I have so much tolerance for the other scoundrels of the world."

A more simple illustration of Dr. Gill's principle is depicted in the comic strip Savage Chickens. I share this with students and parents alike to encourage them to move past shame in order to stretch and grow.

THE IDIOT INTERVENTION

In an "idiot intervention," I invite a parent (or a child) to practice admitting they are an "idiot." This is not a shameful admission, but rather an admission grounded in solid self-esteem. It is acknowledging, "I'm human. I'm flawed. I make mistakes. And I am okay." The experience is liberating and requires us to stand our own imperfect ground.

Many of our students struggle with self-esteem issues and tend to judge themselves harshly. Sometimes they express their low self-esteem in a depressed and deflated way. Other times, surprisingly, it comes across as inflation. A student will respond poorly to feedback, but that fragility will present itself as reactive and angry. He may fight feedback and perhaps tell me that I'm an idiot. I respond by saying, "Yes, I am an idiot, and you're an idiot, and your peers and the staff are idiots also. We're all idiots." Everybody is an idiot. The idiot stance is a position of humility, rather than a position of worth.

Many of history's greatest thinkers have been able to look at their own idiocies. Self-esteem—true self-esteem—is not being convinced of your greatness, but rather accepting that you are still strong and worthy of love in spite of your failings. This position is helpful when somebody criticizes you, as you are neither destroyed by one's judgment, nor do you become defensive. The idiot intervention is one of the best ways to end a debate since you are agreeing with one of your child's most repeated hypotheses.

A way to liberate yourself as a parent is to tell your child, "Okay, I'm an idiot. Now what are we going to talk about? Where does this discussion go from here?"

That puts the responsibility back on the child. If you spend your life trying to be perfect or trying not to "suck," then a couple of things happen. You end up not taking care of yourself, and you set up a dynamic in which your child gets to go around pointing the finger at others for everything that happens in his life and crowing about why it's not his fault. His problems will always be perceived as outside of him.

The idiot intervention encourages people to explore their own shame. The better you are at a certain thing, the easier it would be to explore how you struggle in that area—right? If I am 99.9 percent a great husband, and I'm only 0.1 percent a bad husband, it should be easy for me to face that 0.1 percent. Furthermore, why would I be sensitive to criticism that I am selfish if I am extraordinarily generous? Unfortunately, it doesn't always work that way. Shame is the mechanism that doesn't allow for *any* of our flaws, limitations, or mistakes—but those are things that make up our humanity. Shame hides anything potentially unappealing because it represents the possibility of being rejected, unlovable, or unworthy.

However, none among us is perfect, and we will seldom get it "just right"—whatever that might be.

The following story shows how one mother held herself to a unreasonable standard of perfection. She explained to the group that she and her ex-husband were scheduled to see their son at his treatment facility. "We both try to work together, but we struggle. In the past we have blown up at each other. We are both afraid of each other, and for good reason. There is a lot of water under the bridge, a lot of hurt. We trigger each other, sometimes in front of our son, and we see how that hurts him."

I could sense her helplessness and anxiety. This would be the only time they could visit their son in the next few months, so neither parent wanted to opt out of the visit. After hearing her describe all the possible ways it could go wrong and all the unsuccessful things they had tried in the past, she said, "So tell me what to do so it won't blow up."

My response was not what she expected: "Make a mess of it! Just screw it up." Of course I did not wish for her or anyone in her family to suffer, but I could see how tightly she was holding on to the idea that she needed to get it "right." I wanted to release her from the pressure of managing everyone and everything and direct her toward focusing on what she could control—her choices, intentions, and authenticity. When I explained my intent, her shoulders dropped and I could see the burden she was carrying fall away. When we carry this anxiety, our children learn to reflect it back to us: "Mom, this didn't go well. It's your fault." We teach them to blame us. Think about your intention, but don't measure success by the way your child reacts to that intention or to the outcome.

SHAME-FREE PARENTING

What are some skills we can employ to discourage our children from acting out of shame? It can be helpful to use boundaries to regulate behavior and teach your children. Listen more and avoid moralizing, guilting, blaming, or intimidating them. As parents, we do these things because they show results, because it's easier, and because we like to be in control of other people. But in the long term, such parenting can be devastating.

Avoid leading questions that have a "right answer" when talking with your kids. Try this exercise the next time you're communicating with your children. When you feel the urge to make a statement by framing it in the form of a question, force yourself to do it another way. Instead of sarcastically asking, "Why is it that you did that?" stop and add the words "I'm wondering" before your question.

Avoid the use of imperatives—"you should," "you must," "don't ever." It's hard, and you probably won't be able do this all the time, but try. Once you get in the habit, avoiding imperatives is one of the simplest things you can do. It's not easy but it's simple. I have worked with countless parents who have tried this and come away saying, "I learned so much about the way that I think and relate to people by doing it. I have to consider what I am saying and what I am intending when I require myself to replace imperatives with some other statement."

Listen more. Our own shame and fear, and our subsequent desire to control our children, contribute to poor listening. Instead we lecture, moralize, interrupt, correct, and essentially tell them they're wrong or bad for believing or feeling a certain way. I'll say it again. *Just listen.* Don't give answers. Don't provide solutions. When you listen to your children, they come up with their own solutions. And then, sometimes, when you listen they'll ask you for suggestions.

It takes courage to feel shame, fight it, and do right in the face of it. As we do this work, we will recognize the voices of our fathers, mothers, teachers, priests, peers, and rabbis. When we face our shame head-on, we can learn to reject it and place it where it belongs: in our past. And as we do this, we learn to be more honest with ourselves and others. At times, this process will be lonely. You may lose some people as you break free of this cycle of shame, but by so doing, you will find *yourself* and will then be capable of finding *your people*. Your people are out there, I promise. They are the rare ones. They are the ones who want you to be your true self. They are okay with your worthless, wonderful you.

Children cut out parts of themselves, shoving them in the proverbial closet, in an attempt to find acceptance. Sometimes they fantasize or act out in suicidal ways as they negotiate their shame. I tell them, "*Part* of you needs to die—not all of you—in order to have the life that is waiting for you." Often, what needs to die is the fear of what others think we *should* be doing, which is precisely the driving force of shame.

SHAME IS A BARRIER TO GETTING SUPPORT

What should I tell others about my child's struggles? This question often arises when a family is left to explain where their child is after she has been sent to therapy. Enrolling a child in treatment can temporarily leave a large hole in their family unit, and parents are often challenged to explain this to the community, extended family, or the child's school. Whether or not you have ever been in this situation, as a parent you can likely relate to feelings of loneliness and isolation that come when dealing with a difficult or struggling child.

We hide our story from others for fear of judgment. But when we do that, we also cut ourselves off from many sources of support and connection. The first thing I discuss with families after their child enters our program is that it is their right to tell or not tell anyone about their decision. You are not obligated to tell anyone about the details of your family's struggles. However, I do point out that there is no shame in these struggles and remind them that the mere fact that they are dealing with them head-on is admirable. "Is not our attempt to hide our struggles part of an implicit message that suggests something is wrong with them?" I might ask. We don't consider cancer or heart disease shameful. Why, then, should afflictions such as bipolar disorder, alcoholism, Asperger's syndrome, or depression be any different?

Many parents who are initially reluctant to share their struggles with friends or family are later surprised by the large amount of support that they get once they eventually open up. There are no guarantees about how others will react when you tell them about your trials. Some may judge, disapprove, and/or offer their unwelcome assessment of the cause and cure for your problems. Most parents whom I have spoken to over the years feel validated and more connected with me when I describe to them the struggles I had as a child, a parent, and a person. But others have reacted by saying, "Why should I listen to you? It sounds like you still struggle so much yourself." Frankly, I am glad when people respond that way so they can work to find their own truth, rather than relying on my version of truth.

I would never showcase myself as faultless. I have had some really great moments as a man and a dad, but I have also had some truly low ones. But no one is ideal, and that's exactly what I teach. I would suggest that any wisdom I do have, I acquired through those very struggles. You can't learn from a mistake if you never make one. C. S. Lewis explained this way:

> No man, I suppose, is tempted by every sin. It so happens the impulse that makes men gamble has been left out of my make-up; and, no doubt, I pay for this by lacking some good impulse of which it is the excess or perversion.

Earlier this year, I was contacted by a parent who was considering enrolling her child in our wilderness program. She was interested, but concerned about her family's reputation. "We live in a small community," she said, "and gossip spreads like wildfire. I'm worried about my son's reputation." I reminded her that her son was not worried about his reputation because he was already engaging in negative behaviors.

"It's true," she said. "He likes being known as the town drug dealer.

He likes that he has a reputation and that his profits are tied to how many people know what he does."

"Maybe it's a good thing that everyone knows that about him," I offered. "It might be helpful that adults, schools, and parents know of his history and consider him with a watchful eye. Perhaps that will provide him with extra support and that may prevent him from hiding from others, and thus from himself."

Be cognizant that you are part of this dynamic as well, and it may not be healthy for you to isolate yourself and your problems strictly for the sake of your child's reputation. If you need help and support, and that support will come from sharing your story, then consider doing that for yourself. Finding support in a therapy room or in an anonymous 12-step group can be very healing.

Last, I want to point out that these struggles and disorders are not labels of doom. I wrote my college entrance essay to a strict religious university (BYU) about my difficult teen years, drugs and all. I was accepted, I believe, not in spite of my struggles but because I was able to demonstrate a certain kind of wisdom and maturity that comes from making mistakes and learning from them.

TAKING YOURSELF TOO SERIOUSLY

Being able to laugh at yourself as a parent and recognize your own limitations and your own humanity is evidence of self-esteem. D. W. Winnicott attempted to remove the yardstick of perfection by which parents often measure themselves. He uses the term "good enough" parenting to describe those parents who are "ordinarily devoted." This notion allows us to cut the link between recognizing our mistakes and paralyzing ourselves with guilt. That link, that "blame," causes us to defend, hide, deny, and avoid courageous honesty in our relationships.

Most parents are indeed good enough. Most are neither abusive nor destructive. Most make mistakes but are doing their best. As we develop better self-love, we open up a relationship with our children that allows them to feel and freely express their anger, hurt, and frustration toward us.

Part of your job as a parent is forgiving yourself. It's admitting that you have made mistakes, and then forgiving yourself for those mistakes. Most parents try very hard. Sure, you can be too demanding or too critical at times. But the fact of the matter is that we all make mistakes. You may ask, "But isn't saying that you tried your best and did all you could do a sort of cop-out?" And I will reply, "Absolutely not." Though we make lots of mistakes, we have the courage to address our work and we can still raise children who turn out to be healthy and happy.

Adopting this simple, seemingly contradictory, yet beautiful mantra releases us from the degenerative aspects of guilt and infuses us with powerful motivation to change. When we operate from a place of accountability, healthy detachment, and compassion for both our children and ourselves, we provide them with a safe container in which to grow. They will survive our parenting and become their own amazing human beings.

You are doing the best you can—and you can do better.

CHAPTER EIGHT

BOUNDARIES AND PARENTING

Codependency is co-participation. If we are to contribute to the health of our children, whom we love, then we need to focus first on the relationship with ourselves, then with our children. Only then can we see the relationship we have with our children's problems.

WHEN I TALK TO PEOPLE ABOUT WHAT I DO—WORKING with troubled kids in a therapeutic wilderness program— the most common assumption people make is that the kids come from unloving, uncaring, distant families with little connection or empathy for their children. They envision parents who are just looking to pawn off their children on somebody else. This could not be further from the truth.

Generally, the greater challenge that I see in many families is the inability to detach in a healthy way. Many families we work with present as *overly* attached. This is a dynamic that many of us struggle with on some level. We do not see that the line that divides us is also the line that makes connection possible. It is frightening for us to consider separation as a necessary ingredient in closeness. We fear that we will end up alone if we establish healthy boundaries.

While there are differences between every child and every family, I propose that there are also important similarities. Parents complain that what I teach doesn't apply to them because "my son doesn't do drugs" or "my daughter is older" or "my child has a learning disability." A common struggle in all parent-child relationships is boundaries. Different tools or approaches may be needed depending on the behavior, but the core concept of finding ourselves in the midst of our relationship with our struggling child is still a central topic that requires our attention before we are able to proceed effectively in parenting. The application extends to all our relationships. This chapter explores the concepts of our boundaries with our children and their problems.

CODEPENDENCY OR CO-PARTICIPATION

Codependency and boundaries are difficult ideas to grasp. They are difficult, in part, because the key to understanding them is inside of us. You can't describe or define the principles merely by explaining a behavior. In order to build healthy boundaries, we must be courageously honest and develop precise insight. This is especially true in the face of emotional intensity or in the context of a close relationship. I also would like to introduce the word *co-participation* into the discussion. I will use it interchangeably with "codependency" throughout this chapter and the rest of the book. I like the word because it more aptly describes the phenomenon; we are co-participating in the disorder with our children.

Codependency can be understood by contrasting it with intimacy. Intimacy is the connection two (distinct) people share. Codependency happens when two people share one self. Some people mistake intimacy as that warm feeling we might experience in romantic love. But romantic love, at least in the early stages, is riddled with projections. Thus we are not really in a relationship with someone else, we are just in love with the parts of ourselves we see in them. Of course, the other person helps by hiding those parts of him or herself for fear they will be unappealing. This explains why we often later discover so many unattractive things about our partner that did not seem present during courtship.

While teaching an in-service to our therapists on how attachment theory can inform us in repairing poor attachment for our clients, a therapist interjected, "What I see most in families is overidentification or 'overattachment' rather than a lack of attachment." I explained that overidentification is the most severe form of poor attachment. Over-identification doesn't see the child as an *other*, but rather sees the child as an extension or reflection of the parent. In such a relationship dynamic, there is only one person: the parent. The child is altogether missing in the parent's mind.

Codependency is essentially a lack of differentiation. It is being *too* close to another—so close that there is no space for the other person and their feelings. The term "close" doesn't really describe it accurately because it is actually disconnected. People who struggle with codependency have a lack of self, a lack of boundaries, and overidentification with others and their behaviors. Codependency is an inability to see the line between yourself and somebody else. It's an overreactivity, placing too much emphasis on how somebody reacts to you or what somebody else thinks or feels about you. It's a condition of supporting another's addiction or negative behavior in a complementary role. This is an easy trap to fall into when you have a child who is struggling.

One evening after completing a webinar broadcast in which I addressed a parent's question about how to stay connected to a child enrolled in an out-of-home placement, I walked upstairs feeling a little unsure of myself. I wondered if my perspective was off. At the time, I was dealing with the recent departure of my two oldest children: my son, exploring a service mission back east and my daughter, going off to college. Both had left home within a nine-month span. Although I had been grieving their absence from my day-to-day life, I never doubted that they were both doing the best thing for themselves. So as I listened to this mother's grief in placing her child in a residential care facility, I responded to her question: "I think staying connected isn't about proximity to your child. It is about really seeing them and being connected to what they need. It isn't about having them walk the path with you, but about providing them support so that they might find their own path."

As I came upstairs, my wife was working in the kitchen and I shared my self-doubt with her: "I think my perspective might be off." I explained the question posed to me and my answer to it. "Maybe my family background is just so different. Maybe having Jake and Emma far from home, while normal for me, reflects a kind of disconnection that is not necessarily healthy. Maybe I am just disconnected?" My daughter Isabella, ten at the time, was sitting nearby doing her homework. She interjected without raising her head from her book, "Papa, you are not disconnected. How can you call it disconnected when you are supporting your children to follow their own dreams even though it saddens you to see them go?" How profound and wise. She reminded me that being connected means allowing and encouraging independence.

As my son was preparing to leave on his two-year mission, a right of passage where we would have almost no contact, I found myself suddenly crying at the end of my session in my therapist's office. "I can't find the words to tell Jake how much I love him," I whispered.

My therapist gently assured me, "He knows." Then after pausing for a moment, she added, "And he needs to get as far away from you as he can."

I laughed, relieved, with the realization that she was right. His journey was his, not mine. And a critical part of finding himself lay beyond the boundaries of my life. And my recognition of that was the connection.

Intimacy is hard. It requires tolerance and letting go of the need to control the other person. A number of years ago I was at a wedding dinner, and some of the older people were giving the usual advice to the young couple. One elderly gentleman stood up and said, "If you're not fighting with each other . . . well, then one of you is an idiot." Everyone laughed, and I loved that statement—because it's true. In a family, you are all going to fight and struggle with each other. But your family does not need to be defined by this conflict and struggle, and it doesn't have to prevent you from having a good relationship with one another. On the contrary, if you do the work, then working through the conflict is a path toward individual development and subsequent intimacy.

If my only value comes from helping others work through intense situations, what will become of me if I am not helping others? Parents who struggle with codependency may worry about what will happen when their child becomes an adult: "Will my children still want me in their life if I don't have to solve something for them?"

What happens if people in our life get healthy and don't need us anymore?

WHERE DOES CODEPENDENCY COME FROM?

The concept of codependency was originally established to acknowledge the responses and behaviors that people tend to develop while living with an alcoholic or substance abuser. Since then, codependency has expanded into a term that describes a dysfunctional pattern of living and problem solving that is developed in early childhood years. A codependent person is one who lets another's behavior affect him or her at a debilitating level, and who obsesses over controlling, curing, or correcting that behavior.

Codependency is, in part, an addiction to crisis, drama, chaos, imbalance, stress, and disorder. There is some neuroscience that supports the idea that we can become addicted to the drama of being in an unhealthy relationship. Physiologically speaking, trauma or stress causes the brain to produce the neurochemicals, cortisol, and endorphins regulated by the hypothalamus. When creating these chemicals repeatedly over time, the brain can become *addicted* to them. This is why addicts or members of an addict's family are often unknowingly drawn to drama, intensity, stress, and fear.

We humans develop a remarkable ability to scan our environment. Like an emotional tracking device, we pay attention to the subtlest of cues, the slightest emotional responses, and the tiniest shifts in facial expressions of those around us and adjust accordingly. This type of thinking and these characteristics were hardwired in us so that we could survive our childhood. We developed this way of co-participating with others in an effort to avoid pain, fear, rejection, or isolation. But as adults we don't need it anymore. In *The Drama of the Gifted Child*, Alice Miller writes:

> We then realize that all our lives we have feared and struggled to ward off something that really cannot happen any longer; it has already happened, at the very beginning of our lives.

The development of codependency may start with the reinforcement we receive when we show care for our parents at the expense of our own needs. Then, when we become parents ourselves, we unknowingly require our children to take care of our emotional needs. We reinforce codependent behaviors when we discourage a child's anger and frustration toward us because it feels threatening to us. Over time, the child's worth thus becomes linked to the ways he takes care of others and simultaneously denies any expression that threatens others. We do this as children because the cost is rejection, shame, and abandonment. Put simply, the child equates praise for love and connection. If we do not take on the parents' needs, then we experience their withdrawal of affection.

Usually we are not aware that what we believe about life was instilled in us through countless interactions throughout our childhood. A friend shared a story from Pulitzer Prize–nominated writer David Foster Wallace that humorously describes how difficult it can be to see outside of the context of where you grew up.

> There are these two young fish swimming along, and they happen to meet an older fish swimming the other way, who nods at them and says, "Morning, boys, how's the water?" And the two young fish swim on for a bit, and then eventually one of them looks over at the other and says, "What the hell is water?"

In order to understand your own context, you have to examine and challenge your childhood and your own family of origin. You have to clear yourself of the voices and internalized objects you carry around in your own psyche, in your own internal world. You have to become more conscious of the messages you learned very early on. Sometimes that means taking a few steps back from everyone in your life. Part of growing up and differentiating involves a willingness to look at our own history and background—particularly at our parents—in a critical way.

In the book *The Narcissism Epidemic*, one of the ideas that the authors present is that children who are overly concerned with the approval of their parents and later become parents themselves tend to be overly concerned with the approval of their children. Then, oftentimes, their children will learn that this pleasing behavior is the only way to function in their relationships and they too will search for the approval of others.

DON'T FEEL YOUR FEELINGS

In many families, feelings are not really allowed. This is not usually an overt message, not posted on the refrigerator; it's more of a sense that

Children are often told to look on the bright side, stay positive, to be happy instead of angry or hurt. These mantras arise from an incapacity to watch family members and loved ones suffer and struggle.

certain kinds of feelings or strong emotions are unwelcome.

It is ironic that in some families it's not okay to talk about problems and feelings when the problems might be resolved if only they were discussed. In fact, many times the problem itself is caused by suppressing feeling or emotion. Giving your emotions a name and speaking them aloud becomes the vehicle for *experiencing* your feelings. True communication merely attempts to convey what you are already really feeling. And if you don't properly communicate, your feelings will eventually leak out anyway.

I tell my students, "Be angry at whomever you want. There are going to be standards and consequences for your behavior here, but you have the right to be angry with me. You have the right to hate me. In fact, I would feel honored if you were to tell me I hurt you or you are angry with me. If you swear at me and threaten me and become violent with me, then I'm not going to be honored by that. But your feelings, even if they are negative, are real and important, and I am honored when you share them with me."

The codependent person often has difficulty expressing feelings because of excessive worry about how others may respond. I can relate to that. I once said to my therapist, "Something you said last week really hurt, and I wasn't okay with it. In fact, I carried it around for half the week." She said, "I'm so grateful you told me that. I feel honored. That's the best thing you've done today in therapy." Her response was intimate; and intimacy is honesty. It is two people trying to connect and be whole together. That means that it's okay to sometimes say, "I don't like this. I don't agree with you." With true communication, one person doesn't harbor more power than another in the relationship.

Learning That Your Needs Don't Matter

Because the codependent person has a tendency to place the needs of others first, they suppress their own needs. This often causes boundary distortions related to intimacy and separation that, in turn, lead to anxiety. When you can't properly take care of yourself or ask for help in order to do so, then you steal that self-care from others. I work with students who can't assertively ask for help but end up taking 80 percent of the group's energy on a given day. I also work with parents who won't take care of themselves and who refuse to go to therapy or to a Co-dependents Anonymous meeting but will call me five times a day to ask for help. First and foremost, you have to be willing to help yourself.

Codependency also comes from a belief that taking care of oneself is selfish and wrong. Nothing could be further from the truth.

Jessica Benjamin wrote, "The recognition a child seeks is something the mother is able to give only by virtue of her independent identity. The mother cannot (and should not) be a mirror; she must not merely reflect back what the child asserts; she must embody something of the not-me." If you don't encourage this separation, then you're going to end up stealing from your child anyway. And when you learn healthy self-care, you will also be a more effective parent. Because *Care for your children, but also model independence. Show them it's okay to take care of oneself.* we are taught that others' needs are more important than our own, we have a hard time deciding what boundary or consequence to set with our child. Often, when parents are confused, I ask them to figure out what they need first; the consequences flow naturally from there.

Many parents become so consumed in their role as mother or father that they forget they are living a life themselves. Think of it like the safety instructions on an airplane: Secure your own mask first before assisting anyone else. That's a simple analogy, but it helps to illustrate this point. Take care of yourself and your own health.

RECOGNIZING CODEPENDENCY IN YOURSELF

Because the codependent person often struggles to ask for her needs to be met, she lives instead with the tacit expectation of reciprocity. This often applies to the relationship with our children. We aren't actually being giving when we give with the expectation of receiving something in return. This is true even when all that is expected in return is gratitude. Children can tell, especially as they move into young adulthood, if giving has emotional strings attached. Too often parents send the message that by caring for their sons and daughters throughout their childhoods, they are *owed* loyalty and gratitude in return.

It's okay to say, "If you do drugs, then I'm not going to support you. If you don't get a job, then you're out of the house." That is different. That is setting healthy boundaries and creating clear consequences. But to expect love and devotion from your child out of some concept of reciprocity is to engender codependency.

In codependency there is an emphasis on the external rather than internal world. The outside world can be scary, thus a hypervigilant, scanning stance may be implemented to ensure that nothing will blindside the codependent person. Many codependents suffered through serious dysfunction in childhood, in a home where parents did not provide them protection from traumatic processes or events. And if the children had not developed these protectors in order to function and cope, then the childhoods would have been all the more dire.

When someone is codependent, they take things too seriously and find it hard to laugh at themselves. They think everything is about them. "My child reacted a certain way, my spouse is sulking; it must have been something *I* did." A codependent person tends to take it personally. While we usually associate narcissistic traits with grandiosity, this kind of narcissism is meek. This narcissistic injury was created in a childhood where the child was not seen, nurtured, and attended to adequately.

Codependents have intense fear of being hurt or rejected by others. How others think or feel about them forms their whole basis for their sense of self. This is especially common with parents. In my work I see parents who walk on eggshells and avoid telling their children how they feel for fear of retribution or, even worse, self-sabotage. These kinds of parents are hypervigilant about doing everything "right." They lack assertiveness and clear communication but then carry resentments and frustrations because their children don't respond in the way they want.

I work with many codependent people who say to me, "My son just doesn't respect my things. I wouldn't do that to his things. He doesn't care. He doesn't pick up after himself. He doesn't respond." We think to ourselves, *we* wouldn't act that way, *we* have more respect than that. We judge, and our anger and resentment lingers. Instead of assertively communicating, we blame. Instead of conveying our need for respect, we harbor anger.

One of the things I pay attention to in myself so that I can recognize my own codependency is *obsessing*. When I obsess about what a jerk someone is, or how screwed up someone is, then I know I am sliding down the slippery slope. This is precisely when we need to take a step back and get clear about ourselves and our role in the relationship. The co-participant uses the cloak of how sick the other is to deny that he or she is part of the dance. It is not about the other person, no matter how extreme their behavior may be. It bears repeating that the concept of codependency was developed to help people in alcoholic families, dealing with alcoholic individuals. Drunks surround us, literally and metaphorically, yet their disorder does not mean we have to get into it with them. While the drug addict is intoxicated with a substance, a codependent person is intoxicated by controlling another person.

Obsessing about the other parent's faults or shortcomings is a common occurrence among codependents. When I'm working with a parent, I'll listen to their description of how horrible the other parent is

THE JOURNEY OF THE HEROIC PARENT

once or twice, but when we get to the third time, my response is, "They might be horrible, and they might undermine everything that you do. But you can't change their behavior. You can only change your own. So what are you going to do? What is *your* work? If you were married to someone with schizophrenia, you would probably realize that you couldn't change his or her behavior. But it's the same in this instance. You don't have to be a victim. You don't want your children to believe that we're all just victims of one another." Doing so becomes a distraction to your goal of effective parenting and you are bound to end up fighting battles with your co-parent through your child.

If your child calls you a name, don't call them a name in return. Don't yell and bicker. Instead, set a rule that is not up for discussion. You're the parent. It may not be the best rule, but it's your rule—and that's what matters.

Fighting in lieu of setting a boundary with your child is common in codependency. When I see parents who bicker with their children, it can look more like a peer relationship than a parent-child relationship. The adult lowers himself and his maturity.

The codependent person, to some extent, enjoys self-pity or feels comfortable in that role. Feeling like a martyr is easier, after all, than becoming the hero in your own journey. When you take care of yourself in a healthy way, then you will require respect from others. And if they don't respect you, they don't get to be around you. During a lecture for parents of young adults, a colleague illustrated it this way:

I am invested in a healthy relationship with myself first, and with those that I love next. I am not going to be in a relationship with someone who is abusive. I am not going to be in a relationship with someone who is self-destructive. I love you and want you in my life, but my own peace and mental health are a priority, so if you continue to treat me and to treat yourself in these ways, then I will have to let you go. It will hurt more than I can imagine, but I cannot stay if things continue this way.

When considering our wilderness program, parents will often ask, "What will the outcome be?" And my answer is, "If you do your part as a parent, then we can be 100 percent successful, because that's the only part you can control." From a spiritual perspective, any other answer feeds into the insane notion that we can control another person. Part of what happens for parents as they address their codependency is that they realize the problem is not in their child—or at least they realize that focusing on the problems of their child has actually become the problem—and they need to figure out how to address that in themselves.

At one of our support groups, a father shared a wonderful mantra from his Al-Anon group, which goes, "And maybe it will work and maybe it won't." This kind of practiced detachment illustrates how we can liberate ourselves from focusing on the outcome but not become passive passengers in the vehicle of our own lives.

A key to recognizing codependency is to identify when you tell yourself that others are to blame for your unhappiness or your problems, when you use words like "they make me" or "I have no choice," or "I can't do this or that or it will hurt that person." Richard Bach, in his book *Illusions: The Adventures of a Reluctant Messiah,* illustrates this process with a story. The apprentice challenges the master's comment, "We are all free to do whatever we want to do," by adding, "as long as we don't hurt somebody else," chiding him for leaving off this important qualifier. Then the master conjured up a vampire to illustrate his message. The vampire came out of the forest and asked to suck the blood of the apprentice. The apprentice responded first with terror and then with rage. The vampire was suffering and just wanted a little blood and pleaded with the apprentice for just a little. Then the vampire disappeared and the master asked the apprentice why he did not oblige the starving vampire.

"The thing that puzzles you," he said, "is an accepted saying that happens to be impossible. The phrase is 'hurt somebody else.' We choose, ourselves, to be hurt or not to be hurt, no matter what. It is Us who decides. Nobody else. . . . 'Listen,' said the master, 'It's important. We are all. Free. To do. Whatever. We want. To do.'"

To illustrate the essence of codependency, consider the following story. A young man living in a sober living environment (SLE) was set to come to stay with his mother for the holidays. Earlier that year he relapsed and he had walked the difficult road of earning back the trust of his program. As he prepared for the home visit, he invited his mother to drug test him during his stay. But his mother refused, stating, "I can't do that. If I do it will jeopardize my own recovery from codependency. Your sobriety is yours, not mine. If I naturally discover you're using, I will kick you out. But I am not going to make your recovery my business."

You see that the act is just the act. The boundary problem is inside the mind of the individual committing the act. I told one father who asked me, after his adult daughter asked him, if he should bring cigarettes to her upon completion of our program, "I know you're worried and don't want her to smoke and I can imagine you *bringing* the cigarettes as a gesture that says, 'I am not going to manage this for you.' I can also imagine you *not bringing* them with the thought, 'I can't control whether you smoke but I don't feel comfortable buying and delivering them to you. We can stop on the way to your SLE and you are welcome to purchase some for yourself.'" For codependency or clarity to be revealed, we have to dig beneath behaviors and understand the relationships we have with others and their struggles.

STYLISTIC DIFFERENCES IN CO-PARTICIPATION

The codependent person is often engaged in a number of power struggles. While he is not always going to be angry and demonstrative, these power struggles are always about leverage. They're about conquest and surrender instead of trust, openness, and willingness to feel.

In codependent relationships, people can have strong caretaking impulses. While these instincts seem to be about caring, they are also controlling. Yet codependent people rarely see themselves as controlling. If you find yourself walking on eggshells, being indirect, dishonest, and making the attempt not to offend anyone, then all of this limits your ability to communicate and be yourself, and you are thus exhibiting controlling behaviors. Even though we don't see these kinds of behaviors as controlling, we project that pattern onto others. But these kinds of behaviors are controlling, because the aim is to manage others. If you are spending endless amounts of energy to get a person to react the way that you want them to react—whether that be a child, a friend, or a spouse—that's *caretaking*, and that's controlling.

In my early years as a wilderness therapist, I was working with a young woman suffering from alcoholism. She had been through several treatment facilities prior to ours. As she progressed through our program, she began to express severe anxiety about relapse or regression. While a small amount of anxiety can actually be a good thing in cases like hers— she needed to remain vigilant and humble about the challenges ahead— her anxiety seemed to overwhelm her. As we explored her feelings and their origin, it became clear that she was extremely nervous about losing her father's approval. "He is a rock," she explained. "He has no tolerance for mistakes or setbacks. If he gets upset, he will just cut you off."

"He sounds fragile," I responded.

Incredulous, she corrected me. "No. You don't know him. He is stern and intense. He is very successful and very powerful. I think 'fragile' is the opposite of how I would describe him."

I explained that his inability to endure a difficult relationship and a difficult process, regardless of its appearance, was the epitome of fragility. Sure, he was not a pathetic and helpless creature, but his use of distance demonstrated a profound inability to sit with someone and deal with uncomfortable feelings.

I think she felt validated and was able to understand that his rejections were not about her, but it wasn't until the sad end of her program that we really saw her father's fragility. The young woman shared with her father, after attending graduation week and participating in an overnight experience, that she was feeling anxious about a potential relapse. I had not yet arrived to their campsite for our session and by the time I did her father was gone.

"What happened?" I asked.

"He left after we had an argument, after I shared my feelings about sobriety and my fears about relapsing. He told me I had not made any progress and I just blew up."

The staff informed me that her father had left in a fit. He was angry, wouldn't talk to the staff about what happened, and wouldn't wait for me to arrive. He let them know he would have someone pick up his daughter the next day and that he would call me later. When we finally connected, he was terse and unwilling to discuss his feelings.

I sat with his daughter and a staff member that night under the stars as the daughter expressed her hurt and hopelessness. I reminded her that his rejection and inability to accept her feelings was not about her. I explained how he was hiding his fragility behind anger, judgment, and impatience.

This story illustrates the importance of looking beneath the surface to find our co-participation and our codependent features. They are difficult to identify by behaviors, but are exposed as we see the core feature: the inability to feel and sit with someone else's feelings.

The Legacy of Codependent Parenting

When a child experiences what psychoanalysts call *introjection*, which means swallowing whole the values of another without careful consideration, a person will often do or say something merely because she sees others doing it. Hypercooperative, pleasing, compliant, codependent children are prone to absorb the identities, moralities, and opinions of others in order to bypass the anxiety that can come from having an independent self-identity.

Codependent children often refuse to participate in the task of writing assertive letters to their parents. "My parents were perfect," they might say. "It was all my fault." That's not true, not possible, and not healthy. They will refuse to write what we call "war stories," accounts about their negative behaviors that demonstrate how they were meeting their needs in unhealthy ways. Instead, they immediately say that they are sorry and their behavior was wrong. They say what they think their parents and I want to hear. "I just want to go back to school." "I just didn't appreciate my family."

"Slow down," I'll tell them. "This came on too fast. When you were doing drugs or depressed at home, you saw some sort of benefit in your behavior. At least, you felt a need to engage in that behavior—write from that place. Access that part of you, and then let your parents and me have a look at it and have our own reactions. It's valuable to look at that part of you. That is the part of you that you would prefer to hide in order to avoid rejection or judgment, so it's scary. The problem is that it's very difficult to heal what we do not see and understand. It's true that your parents are probably going to have a hard time with that information once you expose it. But you might try to let go of attempting to control the outcome."

Just as with the stylistic differences in parents, the child raised by a codependent parent may also exhibit a surprisingly tough exterior. Shrinking under the weight of a needy parent, the child may become rebellious. But his rebellion is actually a reaction against the over-whelming stress of taking care of others. And because codependent parenting is actually not close but self-absorbed, there is a lack of empathic connection that contributes to the development of empathy in the child. Many parents of oppositional children are surprised to hear their children described as "anxious to please," but a look beneath the surface reveals the dynamic described here.

The Anxious Parent

Many parents ask children, unknowingly, to take care of them. How? By constantly expressing their anxiety over the child's well-being. When we are anxious about our children's struggles, pain, difficulties, or set-backs, the message is often interpreted as "something is wrong with you" or "you are broken and need to be fixed." This interpretation is damaging because it tends to lead to hiding and suppression. Therefore these children may be more likely to create a defense to distance them-selves from the issue, rather than address it at its roots. A more effective approach is to learn to sit with our children, in their pain, to let them know that they are okay and their pain is okay to feel. From that place they can then work through the issue and access all their resources.

During my son, Jake's, first year at college, he called home to chat. In the course of our talk he shared with me some frustrations he had with a roommate and a teacher, as well as various other challenges. I don't know if it was because he could sense my codependency lurking or because he recognized the pattern from the mistakes in our history, but he ended with this wonderful nugget: "I don't need any help. I will figure it out myself. I just wanted to vent. Thanks for listening."

How beautiful and simple. He let me know how he felt, before I jumped in to "fix" something. Sure, my advice, my anecdotes, or my stories would have been wonderfully crafted! But he was asking for me to sit with my anxiety rather than try to discharge it by resolving something that was not mine to resolve.

The codependent person believes that his love can cure and change another. This is an easy trap to fall into. It's intoxicating to believe in such a powerful notion. The codependent person may be encouraged when they see their child succeeding or becoming "fixed." This makes the codependent person feel integral to the solution and encourages dependence while discouraging growth in the child. It also keeps the child separated from the consequences and rewards of his own life.

We can make mistakes and give ourselves permission to struggle. It may take some work—especially if we grew up in an environment where it wasn't safe to bumble through things. And that's not a cop-out, nor is it a lack of accountability. It is looking at your own humanness, accepting it, and demonstrating for your children that it's okay to make mistakes and acquire the wisdom they offer. It means that you can look at yourself and say, "I am imperfect, but I am still okay. I am doing the best I can, and I can do better."

WILL MY CHILD FORGIVE ME?

This is one of the most common questions parents ask, whether contemplating a child's emotional reaction to a wilderness therapy or any other consequence of significance. Will my child forgive me, will he hate me, will he feel abandoned? These questions tug deeply at the heart of each parent; nothing is so precious as the relationship with one's child, and the fear of losing that relationship is truly frightening.

When my mother told me, "You will love your children more than you will ever love your parents," I felt liberated. I have always felt a pull to reciprocate an infinite amount of love to my mother. But when I compared her expression of love for me with mine for her, I came up short. I believe that we love who we serve, which would explain why we love our children so endlessly. But there are times when we make the mistake and expect that our children should reciprocate our love at the same level of intensity.

So, my response to the question is simply this: Your child will forgive you when he or she gets healthy, because that is what healthy people do. Healthy people forgive their parents for their decisions, for their limitations, for their insecurities, and, surely, for well-intentioned interventions. In that vein, a young person who matures and gains a better-rounded and healthy perspective will forgive a parent (or parents) for initiating an intervention or consequence that they believed was vital to the health, well-being, and, in some cases, to the survival of their child.

Always do your best, because that's all that you can do. Allow your children to have their own emotional responses. Letting go of a child's reaction is one of the greatest contributions you can make to the equation of them moving past resentment toward you. When they realize you are not being held hostage by their emotions and response, they will move toward acceptance, and move away from pressuring, manipulating, and blaming.

MOVING OUT OF CODEPENDENCY/ CO-PARTICIPATION

Moving out of codependency/co-participation is frightening. While we come by this disorder honestly, to move out of it we have to face our fears and self-doubt and realize that we don't need to control to survive anymore. Taking a step back in our relationships with our children is necessary in order to develop a relationship with ourselves. In doing that we will confront our fears of abandonment, rejection, and isolation. We will let go of the grip of control. Our children, especially those who struggle, provide an invitation for us to more deeply explore ourselves, our personal histories, and our relationships with the outside world.

When others try to guilt you back into your old ways of "connecting" in an unhealthy manner, remember that your old ways were not connective.

I think that parents of young adults probably can relate to that pretty well, because they've been living it longer. Detachment is based on the premise that each person is responsible for herself and that we cannot solve problems that are not ours to solve. This doesn't mean that you become inactive. Quite the contrary, it means that you become very active. You set boundaries and present consequences. You do what you know is right and healthy. You let your child make her own decisions, but help her to see what the consequences of those actions might be. Have faith in yourself, in other people, and in the natural order of things in this world. When you detach and are no longer a codependent, then you free the other person and allow her to begin solving her own problems.

> *Detachment is not detaching from the person that we care about, but rather from the agony of involvement in the drama.*

HOW CAN I BE CLOSER TO MY CHILD?

While this question is a natural follow-up to what this chapter discusses, there is a misconception revealed in the asking. Development of the self *must* precede connection and intimacy. To the extent you do not have a developed self, you cannot truly connect with another. Intimacy is the connecting of two people; it is not the fusion of two people.

Our task is first to work on our self, *then* find another self that correlates with yours. My mentor, Dr. Leslie Feinauer, said, "the hardest part of being married is not being with the other person, but being *known* by someone else." Our experience often tells us that if we reveal our true selves, then we will not or cannot be loved. Over the years, I have listened as adults and children have expressed the same basic sentiment in one way or another: "If you really knew me, then you would not—could not—love me." Thus, our first task, developmentally speaking, is to embark on a search for self. We can do this while in a committed relationship, but this may require a partner who is willing to patiently travel that frightening road with us.

The key to healthy relationships begins with each member asking the question, "Who am I?" As who we are becomes more clearly defined, we become more clear about "others" and can more effectively determine our relationship with them. We develop "response flexibility" and move away from old scripts and knee-jerk reactions. We become more connected to others as we are able to move from "who am I" to "who are you." As far as we are able to define the lines that determine who we are and who is the other, we can more confidently understand our relationships. In the case of parenting, as we become clear on who we and our children are, we can then focus on the relationships we have with the child's problems.

This process is the process of developing intimacy in all our relationships. Some time ago a parent asked me the following question: "You are always talking about healthy detachment. When are you going to talk about connection?" This is a great question and led me to this response:

Healthy detachment IS healthy connection.

It is the same thing. Reactiveness or overidentifying with our child is not a connection. In the case of reactiveness we are not conscious or intentional about our response, because our response is rooted in some past trauma or context. Our fears or anxieties lead us to an irrational response that attempts to control the other so our anxiety is reduced.

Viktor Frankl illuminated the difficulty of exposing oneself in psychoanalysis. He said, "The difference between analysis and traditional therapy is that in therapy you talk with a therapist and have to hear them say some really hard things to you. In analysis, you sit with an analyst and have to say some really hard things." But exposing one's real self is extremely important. I learned this from watching one of the children I work with. After expressing something about herself about which she felt very ashamed, her therapist nonchalantly said, "That's okay;

that's how you are. No big deal." My therapist communicates the same message to me when she says, "I don't care if you come in here and tell me you are in love with a duck. You must have a good reason and I want to understand."

The idea here is that true intimacy means that I can be myself; that process is borne of my courage to face the possibility of rejection. It may be fostered by at least one other person telling me that I am okay—no matter what. This does not mean that, as a parent, you are robbed of your ability to set boundaries and expectations for your children, but rather offers light to that process by separating behavior and instruction from love and acceptance.

Share your hurt, your anger, and your dislike. And do it with honesty and a willingness to let the other person have their reaction without feeling like that outcome needs to affect you in a negative way. Intimacy is not always warm or fuzzy, but it is real. Dr. Feinauer once told me, "I don't really believe that my clients trust me until they fight with me. This lets me know they are willing to take the risk to be real and honest."

Parents can follow that same model with their children.

Hearing these things, providing a safe container by not making it about you, and seeing your child's courage in sharing these difficult and sometimes frightening things will demonstrate a healthy detachment and a secure sense of self. This sense of self is not a separate process from connection, but rather a necessary predecessor to connection.

When your child says something like, "I don't trust you," or "I don't think that you're really listening to me," you can say, "Wow, thanks for telling me."

Carl Jung once said, "I would rather be whole than good." Dr. Jung's statement illustrates a common willingness to give up parts of ourselves in order to be labeled with the acceptable moniker of "good." Taking some liberty with this quote, I think I might say, "I would rather be me than fit in." In the Broadway play *Wicked*, Elphaba discovers that her hero, the Wizard, is a fraud. Due to her green skin, she has been an outcast since birth, and she passionately seeks the Wizard's acceptance and approval because she believes that if the Wizard loves her, then everything in her will be healed. When she discovers that he is a fraud, he invites her to collude with him in order to rule Oz through control and deception. In the song "Defying Gravity," she gives her reasoning for declining his invitation and instead taking on the title of "Wicked Witch" and living on her own.

> *Well, if that's love*
> *It comes at much too high a cost!*

The exit from codependence and co-participation comes from developing a relationship with *yourself*. From there you will be able to find and connect to your children and others and can establish a healthy relationship with their problems. Our relationship with others' problems is our responsibility. And when we lose our serenity, it is our responsibility to regain it. Agnes Repplier, the American essayist, put it beautifully and succinctly: "It is not easy to find happiness in ourselves, and it is not possible to find it elsewhere."

THE MYTHS OF
BEING RIGHT

*Rather than possessing an internal sense that we are enough,
we try to be "right" to mask the vulnerability of owning it, which
leaves us alone on a psychological island by ourselves.*

ANYONE WHO KNOWS ME WILL ATTEST THAT I KNOW A LIT-
tle bit about the seduction of being "right." Often people try to
be right so they don't have to deal with the more vulnerable
aspects of relationships. Wars are waged over "rightness." Each lays
claim to their side and clings to their unassailable "right" position. Both
sides end up bruised and bloodied.

Parents are no strangers to the "I'm right" game. They think that if
their child is wrong (using evidence their children amply provide), then
they are justified in taking a certain stance. This chapter will discuss
the psychology behind claiming themselves "right." I will touch on a few
areas where this mind-set is harmful in parenting. We will also explore
alternative ways of relating to our children and their problems, and I
will present a process that I hope will provide both parents and children
a sense of liberation.

WHY DO I NEED TO BE RIGHT?

As time goes on, it seems I work harder each year to set my boundaries and make my preferences known. When I discuss these with someone else, I'm not saying they're wrong; rather, I'm saying, "Here is what I want. Here is what I need. I don't know if I'm right, and I definitely don't know if you're wrong, but I know this is what I want and need." That's the goal. As a parent, you can talk about your needs and communicate them, and in turn you want your child to do the same. You determine what is right for you, but be cautioned: this does not make you right.

Because of my training in diagnostics, it's easy to see faults in those close to me. If I allow myself, I can find faults in everybody. Indeed, if I allow myself to go down that road, I can even see seemingly benign interactions as pathological. It doesn't take tremendous talent to find fault in another, and I have perfected it. It's something I do out of weakness. It's something I do because I don't feel strong enough to say, "This is what I believe, and I might be wrong. This is my boundary, and this is what needs to happen for me to make this work."

The goal is to connect to yourself, find yourself, and to be okay with yourself, so you can allow your children to do the same. The greatest thing in the world is to be seen and acknowledged by another, because when you're truly seen by somebody, then there's a chance you can find yourself. Jessica Benjamin put it this way: "Recognition is that response for the other which makes meaningful the feelings, intentions, and actions of the self."

WILL BEING PERFECT OR "RIGHT" PREVENT MY CHILD FROM STRUGGLING?

I constantly remind the children in our program that their parents are only human and thus imperfect. "In spite of that fact," I'll tell them, "it's your responsibility to be healthy. No one in your life is ever going to be perfect—not your teachers, friends, siblings, boss, spouse, or me. But that doesn't give you an excuse to be an ass or give up."

Conversely, I warn parents of the dangers and pitfalls of trying to "get it perfect" in our relationships with their children and with others. There is great danger in the perfection mentality. As much as we can and should aspire to be ethical, moral, and healthy, we can never be perfect. It is important as a parent to challenge the idea that you have to be right or good all of the time.

For example, I work with many parents whose children experience addiction problems, and they ask me, "Since my child is struggling with drugs and alcohol, do I have to be sober in order to create boundaries?"

My response to that is typically "No. If you're drinking too much, or if you're using drugs, then we can talk about that as a separate issue. But if you're thinking about not drinking strictly so that your child will not have an excuse to drink, then you are shifting *their* accountability onto yourself. In other words, you are creating a culture in your family that says your child cannot be held accountable for his actions unless *you* do everything right too."

Sometimes, as parents may be trying to resolve patterns from their own family of origin, they might think, "I don't want to do what my father or my mother did, or follow the way I was raised, so I'm going to act like this." This can also be a dangerous way of thinking. You may end up creating a split when your desire to act differently from your parents blinds you to some of your own faults. You may not see the similarities between you and your parents, or the limitations in yourself. I urge my clients of all ages to have the courage to look honestly at those parts of themselves that are buried beneath shame. One of the consequences of suppression is projection. When we begin projecting our feelings and behaviors onto others, including our children, then we stop seeing *their* needs. We try to solve the problem outside of us when it is really within us and rooted in our history.

Several years ago, I saw a touching example of this unfold between a sweet son and a loving father. During a session in the woods, the father explained through tears the pain he felt from the distance that had grown between him and his son. "I always took you out to play catch; I always took you to ball games. This was something that my father never did for me, so I wanted to do those things with you, but it hasn't been working."

"But I never liked sports, Dad," the son responded. "I like art, music, and reading. You weren't connecting to me then; you were trying to connect with your own dad."

We have to be careful when running away from our family of origin. Instead, try to understand the root of your resentment and unresolved issues with your parents. Get to a place where you can say, "My own mother and father had strengths and weaknesses, and I'm going to forgive them for their weaknesses and be thankful for their strengths." Don't move too quickly toward forgiveness, though. In almost all instances, if you move too quickly, you end up continuing to repress your hurt and anger; ultimately it leaks out, oftentimes onto your own children. While forgiveness is a healthy part of spiritual transcendence and a fulfilling and joyful life, if you don't do the work and experience the hurt that comes before forgiveness, then you're likely to end up with repressed emotions. Taking time to work through difficult experiences in your life means you acknowledge and respect those parts in yourself.

As parents, we often think that our feelings are not enough, and that merely communicating the way we feel is a pointless endeavor. We find some study, proof, expert, scripture, or theologian to show that what we are saying is true and valid. This, however, is a tenuous place to be, because when you appeal to that outside authority, your child can then simply appeal to someone else who may hold an opposing theory. But when you speak from your heart and use "I feel" statements, your child cannot argue. "This is what I think. This is my experience. This is what I feel. This is what I believe." These are *your* feelings, and you don't need any authority to validate them; they are absolute.

In turn, our children have a right to think and feel anything they want. They have the right to think you are a horrible dad or that the consequence you just gave them is stupid. And ideally, if you are feeling good about yourself, you can listen to those feelings, connect to them, and understand where they are coming from without being offended and needing to correct or disprove.

This morning, while writing this chapter, I took a few minutes to snuggle with my youngest, who I brought with me on a trip. I thanked her for coming with me and asked her, "How do you like your 'only child' vacation?" She is the youngest of four and sometimes finds that hard. Olivia responded, "I wish I was an only child." My first inclination was to respond with a list of benefits of living in a family with her brother and sisters. I think most parents would at least feel this impulse, if not act on it, if their child expressed such a sentiment. But luckily I was writing this book, so my mind was in a good place and I agreed with her. We talked about all the ways it would be better for her if she were an only child. We talked about how little attention she gets at times because she is just one of four children in our family. She seemed relaxed and she then finished the story by expressing gratitude that her siblings do play with her sometimes. By letting her have her truth, she had ultimately come around to the same conclusion that I had hoped she would.

IS THERE A RIGHT WAY TO EARN OR GIVE TRUST?

A lot of parents feel as if they owe their children trust, and I don't think that's always true. Trust is *given*. Yes, some trust "too easily" while others struggle trusting anyone. These polarized aspects of trusting likely point to some buried history that is worth exploring. I have often challenged parents whose trust issues seem to be coming from some other place. An example of this would be a father I worked with who grew up with an abusive alcoholic mother. His response to his son's slow recovery from substance abuse was cruel and sarcastic. While my general rule is to support parents in where they are with their trust with a child, I saw this father's responses as clear evidence of his own history and intimacy with someone afflicted with addiction.

I tell my students, "We may not give you the trust that you deserve in different areas of this program, and that's going to be tough for you. If you're accountable, you'll tolerate this lack of trust, but if you're not accountable, then you might become pretty indignant about it. Your tolerance for the reactions of others is a good indicator of whether you're doing the work to impress people or doing the work for its own sake." This is how you get a sense of where children stand with their own accountability.

Forgiveness and trust are yours to give. Your child doesn't get to demand it.

I once worked with a client who was a chronic liar. We treated him as being addicted to lying, but the underlying issue was control. While in the wilderness, this young man got a letter from his parents accusing him of stealing his mother's heirloom watch and pawning it. After reading the letter, I asked him about it, and he confessed. "Yeah, I stole the watch and sold it," he said. "I bought something for my girlfriend, and I used the rest of the money just being the cool guy and buying things for my friends." Afterwards, I acknowledged his honesty and courage in admitting something he'd been holding onto and lying about for a while. Two weeks later, his mom found the watch. It had fallen behind her dresser. Initially this mother felt terrible guilt for accusing her son of something he didn't do, even though he had demonstrated a profound pattern of lying, giving her plenty of reason to be suspicious. I asked her to consider forgiving herself and told her that if her son were accountable, he would easily forgive her.

She talked to me about it on the phone and she wrote a letter to her son under my direction. She asked him why he lied about stealing and selling the watch, and he said, "I wanted people to trust me, so I lied so that people would think that I was trying to be honest."

Another week went by, and his parents found something else that had gone missing, but they were afraid to accuse their son. Stealing was indeed one of his patterns, but his parents had wrongly accused him once already. Still, I told them, "He has stolen from you many times before. He has betrayed your trust. Even if you don't know about all the details, or even if you can't prove it, you still have the right to share your experience with your child."

When we think about trust as an objective, conditionally earned reward, we learn to deny our feelings and experiences. I encourage parents to explore the trust they feel for others and own it. It is theirs—and they don't have to defend their level of trust to their child. Arguing that the way we trust is "right" leads family members to believe that trust is some kind of objective level that we find, instead of something we *feel*. Even if the mistrust originates from something other than the current situation, those feelings will ultimately lead to identifying something important.

WHEN IS THE RIGHT TIME TO FORGIVE?

Many parents ask, "When should I forgive? When has the scale tipped enough to forgive and move on and not be angry?" Sometimes I help people who are stuck in their anger and resentment to forgive and move on. I move in this direction when the client and I have discovered that this lack of forgiveness either stems from some other place, or that it has become a sort of defense to guarantee they will never be hurt again. Yet most of the time I tell them, "You have the right to feel what you feel as long as you feel it."

One adolescent student I worked with became indignant because his mother had found a bag with some white powder residue under his bed and she then accused him of using cocaine. "How dare she?"

Artificially letting go and forgiving because you feel that you should or because you think you must can be a dangerous thing for both you and your child.

he asked during one group session. After he finished his self-righteous rant, another student asked what was in the bag. "Heroin," he answered. Surprised by the irony, I let out a laugh. His mom had accused him of using the wrong substance, so for that he felt justified in denying accountability for his actions. This young man, at that point in his life, did not know what trust meant.

As I mentioned earlier in this book, I have heard the advice "don't go to bed angry" given to many newly married couples. This is some of the worst advice that you can give, in my opinion, because it encourages us to deny our feelings. It is absolutely okay to go to bed angry. I have seen many cases of domestic violence result in part because the couple is unwilling to tolerate a lack of resolution. When you don't take time away from each other, the situation escalates. It's okay for you to step back and decipher how you feel. It's okay to feel angry, hurt, and sad. I know that it's sometimes uncomfortable and even frightening. But those feelings stem from anxiety, and you need to give yourself time to experience your feelings.

DEALING WITH A CO-PARENT'S "WRONGNESS"

This is one of the most challenging issues I address when talking with struggling parents. I am often asked whether I think a parent should take legal action against their co-parent—custody changes, divorce, court orders for treatment, etc. Most of the time, the conflicts or differences in opinion parents describe are not serious enough to warrant or justify legal action. Courts are reluctant to intervene with a parent's rights. Termination of parental rights is a very serious intrusion into the family, and it usually only applies in cases of severe neglect or abuse. I think it's a good idea to consult with a family law attorney in your state to understand what your options are even if you don't decide to take further action. Doing this can create a sense of liberation and freedom when you feel like you and your child are victims of a toxic partner.

Many parents, both married and divorced, feel that the co-parent undermines the values they are trying to model, teach, and demonstrate. The co-parent may be sending unhealthy messages or engaging in unhealthy or enabling behaviors. Parents are often tempted to send private e-mails to their therapists or spend a great deal of energy listing the negative actions and attributes of their co-parent. This attempt to place blame often becomes a distraction, especially for the one making the complaint. In doing so, parents can lose some clarity in various ways.

First, they lose the clarity in distinguishing between co-parent and child. Failing to separate the attributes of the co-parent and the child, even if there are indeed similarities, is a slippery slope. It blurs the line between how the co-parent has hurt you and how the child has hurt you. Murray Bowen calls this dynamic *triangulation*. In family systems theory, whenever two people have problems with each other, one or both will "triangle in" a third member. Rather than talk with her husband and deal with her frustration with him, a new mother might preoccupy herself with her child. In this case, the wife diminishes her anxiety by ignoring its source (the relationship between her and her husband); the husband is on the outside while the wife and child are on the inside.

Even as I say all this, I will acknowledge that I have communicated negative messages about my own wife to my children through eye rolling, subtle jokes, teasing, or even a suppressed emotion showing on my face. Obsessing over a co-parent's faults, how to change or convince them, or even dwelling on the negative effects of their behavior on your children is a hallmark of codependency. A professor of mine once said, "What you tell me about the devil tells me more about *you* than it does about the devil." When you're obsessing over your co-parent, it suggests you are spending too much energy on finding their faults and don't have enough energy left over to work on your own.

Even when your child comes to you complaining about their other parent, you are almost never the best one to contain it. Respond with empathy and encourage your child to work it out with the other parent directly, or with a therapist. Part of the problem when our children come to us with these situations is that we often *like* it. It validates feelings toward the other parent, and we may feel as though we are abandoning our child if we don't join in with her complaints. However, utilizing the simple responses above and coupling that with "I am not the best person for this discussion because it is clouded by my own relationship with your mother" is a healthy way to support and redirect your child while still keeping your own boundaries clear.

The most common feature I see in these dynamics is the propensity for a parent to polarize with the co-parent. It is common in many families I see for one parent to focus on the co-parent's weaknesses in the hopes of compensating for them in their own behavior. For instance, if a mother feels like her husband is not nurturing enough toward their son, she might try to make up for it by enabling the child. Or, on the opposite end of the spectrum, a father might think his ex-wife enables their daughter and allows her to get away with too much, so he might sacrifice nurturing and connection with his daughter in order to create more structure. Sometimes a mother or father will even start parenting in a way that he or she doesn't agree with, simply to counterbalance the other parent's actions. In such cases, it is the *child* who becomes lost. The child's best interests are not being considered because the parent is spending all his energy on trying to balance his co-parent.

Bowen suggests working through the *original* conflict. In other words, you must sort out your anger and hurt with your co-parent in order to avoid the trap of seeing his or her problems in your child. Co-parenting therapy is ideal in such cases, but sometimes there is too much hurt, distrust, and a lack of equal commitment to doing the necessary work. So what else can you do? Plenty. Attend a support group.

Talk to a therapist or a friend. If necessary, take legal action. Don't talk negatively about your co-parent with or in front of your child. Set the course to be the best parent you can be to your child. Be generous with your child by admitting *your* weaknesses. Stay connected to yourself and look for balance within. Doing all this will create a sense of safety for your child and allow them to see it is okay to be imperfect. Be a model for your child to confront her own limitations. You can still provide one of the greatest sources of resiliency for your child—to have at least one adult in their life who sees her.

OWNING AND EXPRESSING YOUR NEEDS

Expressing yourself in terms of what you need is one way to avoid power struggles and debates over right and wrong. It's okay to ask for what you need. Years ago, I decided to abandon the age-old battle of trying to convince my children that my way was the right way. "I am sorry, kids, I know I struggle with OCD, but we are going to have to work this way. You can keep your room as messy as you like, but the common areas have to be to my specifications." You see how this is changing it from a debate to an assertive request and stance. It is not, "This is a pig sty and unhealthy and unacceptable," but rather, "Your dad is a little crazy, so we are going to have to work with him a little." That's not being autocratic and disrespectful. Rather, it is being assertive. It's about feelings, requests, boundaries, and self-respect.

There are fewer things more disconcerting to our children than when we talk about things in terms of "should" and "the right way" instead of what we need. They can sense that we need things and that they are being used or manipulated, but they can't express it. If we openly acknowledge our needs, our children won't have to sacrifice themselves at our expense.

It is okay to express yourself as a parent in terms of what you need. In fact, it is validating and liberating for your children.

THE JOURNEY OF THE HEROIC PARENT

I have a very close friend who underwent a battle with cancer. I did everything I could to be there for him, but I had to be careful that I wasn't turning this experience into what *I* needed. There were times when my friend needed space. He needed me to take care of my fears, my grief, and myself so he didn't have to. He told me stories about how people would come to visit him during his chemotherapy weeks. He was too sick, too weak for the visits, but the visitors needed him to know that they cared about him. In this perverse way, they were selfishly asking the cancer patient to take care of them. He didn't need—or even have the ability—to take care of others then. Similarly, I have seen parents provide updates to loving family members on their child's progress in our program, only to come away confused about why these interactions left them feeling drained. They had to learn to ask for what they needed: "I know you are concerned and care about Susie, but I need some space. I will send out one e-mail each week to all of you so I can better take care of myself."

MODELING SELF-CARE

My therapist shared the following story with me about her son in order to illustrate the idea of healthy self-care for both parent and child. One summer she planned to visit her son. She confirmed everything as the date drew closer, and was excited for the trip. But when she arrived in Boston on a Thursday afternoon, she received a voicemail from her son informing her that he would not be available until Saturday afternoon. Her son was not crawling on the ground and begging for forgiveness, but rather assertively explaining his need to take care of some personal business. A big client was in town, and it was her son's obligation to host the client and accompany him to several meetings. She realized that she would be by herself for half the trip. But instead of feeling resentment, she felt happy for her son. She was happy that he could take care of himself and that he felt safe enough to assert his needs. She did not guilt him; she did not remind him of their plans. She responded by telling him to take care of himself, that she would enjoy the time to herself in the city, and that she looked forward to seeing him when he was free.

You have to go out there and get what you want. You have to tell people, "This is what I like. This is what I'll tolerate. Here's what I'm okay with." Again, at first, when people make this shift to taking care of themselves, it may come across as forward or even obnoxious. Eventually, though, our comfort with the skill increases and we learn how to express our needs firmly but without alienating or offending the other. So take care of yourself enough to be an asset to your children, and so they don't have to take care of you. Otherwise you become an emotional liability.

MODEL STRENGTH IN YOUR VULNERABILITY

Many parents and people in positions of authority find it hard to be vulnerable and admit to struggling. I'm not talking about taking some kind of helpless victim stance, but about simply being self-aware and humble enough to admit weaknesses. While it's hard to say to my child, "I didn't do this well, and I'm struggling with this," one of the most effective ways of responding to your children is by sharing a similar situation with which you might be struggling. Peer pressure is an example I use over and over again. I can't tell you how many times parents have shared wonderful little lectures on peer pressure that almost never work. However, if you're honest, you might approach it by saying, "I struggle with peer pressure too. It might be more complex, and I've made some progress since I was sixteen, but I still pay attention to the car that I drive and what I wear." Guess what happens when you do that with your children? They actually get inspired. They begin to see the similarities between you, rather than the differences. Seeing similarities in others, even when there are vast differences, is evidence of mental health.

When you do this, when you don't make the situation about yourself,

Find your own mirror; stop using your children to show you that you're okay.

then you will become a better listener. You won't feel the temptation to tell them why you're right and why they're wrong. When your child is upset with you, or when he's hurt, listen to him and stop turning it around so that he feels he has to take care of you. That will be especially important as the relationship moves forward. As a bonus, you model willingness to take risks and own the outcome, good or bad. This is a skill that will serve both you and your child well, should they choose to follow your example.

HIDING OUR FEELINGS BEHIND THE MASK OF "RIGHT"

As I mentioned, I have struggled in my life to be right and to make other people feel wrong. Being right is about as satisfying as empty calories; it's the fast food of relationships. There's no sustainable nutrition there, nothing healthy. Instead, it is only a way of discharging our unwanted feelings onto another person so we don't have to feel them ourselves. "If you are wrong or bad, then I don't have to feel hurt or sad. I just pronounce judgment and stand back with my indignation at your faults." One of the hardest things to do in a relationship is simply to say, "I feel hurt. I feel scared. I feel sad." That is a very difficult place to stand.

Just being yourself and having that be enough is hard for parents. We all have deficiencies and insecurities, but that's why we go to therapy, that's why we read self-help books, that's why we learn and ask ourselves tough questions. Use the "I" statements: "I think," "I feel," "I believe," "I want." This is the most powerful way to communicate. When we make others wrong, when we throw out insults or judgments, we rarely get anywhere. But when we share our relative feelings, we have a better chance at being heard and are less likely to provoke a debate or a defense. This departure from "you" to "I" is what makes the difference.

As a father and a therapist, I often ask myself, "How do I take down this mask of 'rightness,' this defense, and how does this relate to a healthy self-esteem?" I have come to conclude that a fundamental ingredient to a healthy self-esteem is being "seen." This doesn't necessarily mean being loved or cared for, but rather feeling understood. As we discussed earlier in the book, the essence of the self is usually found through someone else. So if someone else finds us, then we have a chance to find ourselves. We've all experienced that moment where somebody "got" us, somebody empathized, somebody understood. Even in our perceived craziness, we felt found, recognized, validated, strong, and okay.

An important aspect that allows us to compassionately look at our symptoms or wounds is to experience that compassion in the person of another. Ideally, this is the mission of a therapist. They can say, "I can tolerate you. You are enough." And when we can be enough, then we don't have to engage our child in the debate over who is the bad one and who is the good one. So many couples come to marital therapy with this same agenda. They come in complaining, trying to prove that the other one is the sick one.

This is part of what therapists mean when they talk about the *identified patient dynamic*. We have the patient, sometimes extremely symptomatic, and then we have the other members of the system. Neither is causing the other to act in a certain way. There is no need for blame or causality, yet there is a culture and a dance in the family. Part of creating a place where everyone can be vulnerable, feel what they feel, and own their part of the dance without shame removes the need for a system to have a "sick one" altogether.

Salvador Minuchin, a pioneer in family therapy, staged an intervention that I have borrowed many times. He was treating children and adolescents at the Philadelphia Child Guidance Clinic. After an initial session with a family he invited them to participate in the following ritual on the way home. Stop off and have an ice cream. Buy your daughter any ice cream she wants. Tell her she is fired—fired from being the identified patient. Tell her that no matter how healthy she gets that you will work on yourself, your parenting, your communication, and your listening.

For the first several years I presented webinars, the last slide of every presentation read "this is not cause and effect." I included that slide because I got a lot of feedback about how parents felt guilty after watching. I was just teaching parenting skills and principles. But as parents watched the lectures, they took a mental inventory about how well they were doing and came to the conclusion that their child was struggling because of *their* mistakes. That was not my intention, nor did it reflect my belief about those parents. I added that slide to remind them (and me) that the training is not about them being perfect in the hopes of their children being perfect. It is about providing them with some tools that give them an opportunity to participate in the most rewarding thing I have ever experienced, a connected relationship with one's child.

CHAPTER TEN

HOW TO GET THE SUPPORT YOU NEED

What surrounds you in life is a manifestation of what you think you deserve. It won't work to "ask" to be treated a certain way by others; we have to require it in order to get it.

FEELING HOPELESS AND ALONE

Families dealing with difficult children often feel helpless, hopeless, and alone. They come to our parent support groups to be reminded of principles and skills, but they also come to simply sit in a room with other parents who understand. They want to be able to tell their story and not be judged. A mother recently shared, "I had so many judgments about others, and then I found myself sitting in my car at two a.m., crying and alone, not wanting to go home to face my child, who had been expelled from school earlier that day. I was embarrassed and didn't want to face my neighbors."

Dealing with children often invites a new perspective, one that is hard to get any other way. A father shared, "This experience has changed the way I look at homeless people. My son, now twenty-three and suffering from mental health and addiction issues, could end up that way. I see a homeless person and I see my son. I used to ignore them and would never offer them anything. Now I make eye contact, say hi, and offer a hand in support."

This feeling of isolation is also borne out of the grief about the way things "should have been." The judgments kept us guarded and gave us a sense that "it would not happen to us." Raising children can crack us open to receive new lessons and awareness. Parents of struggling children don't need simple solutions or advice, but rather understanding and community. They need to feel willing to shed their old life and its illusions of "should" in order to develop a sense of empowerment and hope. Part of this journey is about letting go of old ideas and sometimes letting go of people, of all their advice and judgments. The journey is about practicing self-care so we don't ask our children to be responsible for taking care of us.

Working your way through the journey this book describes will change you. Good therapy or parent education does not offer the *answer*, but rather provides the participant with tools and support for discovering his truth. Understanding this, and surrounding yourself with people who understand this, is infinitely rewarding and will sustain you through life's trials.

ADDITION BY SUBTRACTION

Let's start off this chapter with what we *don't* need in our lives. We don't need experts with simplistic solutions. Of course, an expert can guide you to find your truth, to travel your own journey, experimenting and learning as you go. Parenting tools ask you to stretch and grow. But uninvited advice offered from on high does more to shame a parent than inspire him. New therapists often focus on symptoms and diagnoses to the exclusion of connecting to others. The "PhD disease" shows itself when your new therapist believes he has it all figured out. After all, he is wading into new waters to try and help people. It takes time before he realizes that authenticity, vulnerability, and deep listening are the healing forces in therapy. Right out of graduate school, I remember being very clear about everyone else's problems, including my own family and friends. I had diagnoses and evidence-based advice at the ready for any willing (and unwilling) participant. It wasn't until I got in touch with the wisdom of *not* knowing that I truly began to understand therapy. This wisdom came as I explored my own pain, both self-created as well as the uninvited pain that life inevitably offers.

Creating an environment that nurtures you requires that you set boundaries. You tell friends and family what you need and what you don't. In some cases, family and friends will even meddle to the point that they undermine your boundaries by talking about you disrespectfully to your children. Or they will provide your child a soft place to land instead of dealing with the consequences of her actions. In these instances, you will be tempted to argue or prove yourself to others. You will want them to agree, but your only real defense against such intrusions is a boundary: "I am sorry you feel this way and need to share it with me each time we talk, but I am going to ask you to keep your opinions to yourself. If that doesn't work for you, I can't allow you in my life right now. That is not my preference, but it is what I need to do to take care of myself—especially at a time where we are going through some challenges." A boundary is a boundary is a boundary. Threatening, pleading, arguing, and bullying are not boundaries.

In order for us to surround ourselves with people who can love and support us in the way we need, we have to first require it of them. This applies to family, friends, and professionals. It is scary and will bring up feelings of guilt, but in order to create a safe context for ourselves we will have to fight the old messages that tell us we *have* to be loyal or obligated to someone, even when there is a well-established pattern of mistreatment.

ADDING LIGHT TO OUR LIVES

Now that we have addressed some things we need to discard in order to change our contexts, let's talk about what we can *add* to give our lives more meaning. The two categories I want to focus on are empowering messages, and ways in which we can practice better self-care.

Empowering messages are things we remind ourselves of in order to experience liberation. We have to challenge old scripts by replacing them with mantras that give us permission to do what we think is best. This is not easy since many of the old messages are hardwired into us. It is difficult to adopt new ideas because the old ideas are embedded with guilt—guilt that we are betraying our families, our friends, or ourselves.

Here is a discussion of some parent rights that I have found helpful (adapted from *Teen Tips* by Tom McMahon). It is critical to understand that these rights are for *you* to internalize. Some parents will try to sell these to their child, hoping the child will support them, but this, like everything else, will likely devolve into a debate. If you try to justify them to your child by saying, "Honey, look, I have a right to consult other people, and this is why..." then you're opening it up to discussion. I hear people say, "He can't say that or treat me that way." And my observation is, "It seems like he is treating you that way. What can you do to make sure that doesn't happen again?" Your rights in the matter don't get to be discussed and debated.

> **When you make mistakes or when you change your mind, you're still "good enough." You don't have to get everything perfectly right.**

Parents have the right to make mistakes. When they do make a mistake, they sometimes believe their credibility is shot. But with this mentality, admitting to a mistake is going to be very difficult. If you change your mind, you'll worry your child will use that against you.

You have a right to take time to make a decision. You don't have to decide everything all at once, especially in a situation when you and your child are getting heated. We are tempted to lie when we think that setting a boundary will lead to a battle. I remind parents that it's okay to let your child know that a decision has been made but that you don't want to talk about it yet. You have a right to say, "I want to think about it before I answer," or "I don't want to talk about that."

You have the right to be authoritative when logical explanations have not succeeded. Part of a healthy family is an appropriate hierarchy. Sometimes we are afraid to stand our ground. Doing so can be lonely, and many of us still hold on to resentments toward authority figures in our own early life experiences.

Remember that as a parent you have the right to consult professionals or other adults. I have heard many children tell their parents, "You're weak. You're only saying what your therapist says"—and I've seen this trigger many parents. But it is helpful to remember that you have the right to seek outside help, and there's nothing weak about it. In fact, it's the opposite. When you seek outside help to do something you don't know how to do, you are showing your strength and resolve.

You are also allowed to ask your therapist tough questions and challenge them. When parents participate in our program, we believe it's the therapist's responsibility to be patient with them, listen to them, answer their questions, and be nonjudgmental. We also believe that you have the right to ask your therapist the same questions over and over again. You have the right to disagree with a therapist, a parent coach, or this book. If the response is shaming, frustrating, or judgmental when you challenge a therapist, you have a right to end the conversation.

As you make these changes in your life, you will learn that your child can adjust to your newfound confidence. However, it is important to remember that people don't initially always celebrate our growth. It is sometimes difficult when someone we love sets a boundary with us because it is new and maybe even scary. Some parents want to take what I teach and in turn present it to their kids so that they will be okay with their new version of parenting. I imagine you may think that if you say some of these things to your children or other members of your family that it would be like a bomb exploding! In the end, embarking on a journey toward valuing yourself can lead to you having a more supportive group of friends and family.

THE UNLIVED LIFE OF A PARENT

Selfless parenting is an idea that some parents believe they are sworn to live by, a belief that says, "I do everything for my child. Their needs come first, and mine come second or not at all." Though this kind of thinking may seem admirable, carrying it out is almost impossible. And it is likely not healthy for either one of you.

Believing that you can parent in a completely selfless way creates many traps. First, it reinforces a lack of empathy. It is important to be assertive with your child and tell him or her, "I matter, and my feelings matter." Are you both showing and requiring empathy in your home? Are you making sure your child knows that you are a person who has valid feelings? If not, then your child's "center of the universe" way of thinking is probably being reinforced.

You might say, "Well, Brad, you're trying to teach us that we should become totally selfish and that we shouldn't care about the children. I believe that a child, especially when they're young, *ought* to be nurtured and taken care of." Look, I don't want you to flip to the other end of the continuum and become completely apathetic to your child's needs. It is important to find balance. But if you hold on to the idea that every breath you take is for your child, then you are not modeling self-love and self-care. A friend of mine who teaches a course on de-escalation and self-defense sums it up with this quip: "If you can't keep yourself safe, you can't keep the other person safe."

The word "selfish" carries a negative connotation. When we feel that we're acting selfish, we are judging ourselves, and we often pass that negativity on to our children. We use the word "selfish" when we want to punish others or try to control their behavior. People tell us we are selfish when we don't do what they want us to do. The idea of calling someone selfish is often an attempt to get the other person to take care of our needs.

Try eliminating the word "selfish" from your vocabulary when thinking about your parenting. Talk about being ineffective; talk about goals; talk about the benefits of behavior and choices; but don't talk about selfish versus unselfish. When you attempt to act as a selfless parent, you create an unhealthy dynamic in which you must get your needs met through your child. When you parent in this way, you are *using* your child rather than connecting with her. When you don't value yourself, then you don't model self-care (and self-worth) for your child. If you're a selfless parent, where is the space for your child to be angry with you? A great deal of guilt can grow within a child if her parent needs to be completely selfless.

Many of the students who come to our wilderness program are depressed. They have engaged in self-harm or self-destructive behaviors. Essentially, what we teach them is how to care about themselves. I often say to my students, "I want you to be selfish. I don't give interventions with the goal of ruining your life. The goal of any intervention is to create an experience that is going to benefit you."

When students ask, "What's in this for me?" I don't respond by scolding them for being selfish. They have a right to ask how something is going to benefit them. At the same time, I try to teach my students about the rewards that come from caring for other people, helping them, having empathy, and being connected.

In our program, I often ask students, "How did your parents hurt you? How did they affect you negatively?" Many of them respond by saying, "Well, my parents didn't do anything wrong." And I'll say, "That's not realistic. Every parent makes at least *one* mistake. It doesn't make them a bad person, nor does it make them a bad parent. And it's okay to be mad at them." Your child needs to know that being mad or sad is okay.

When they become mad at you, they needn't feel that it will destroy your self-worth because your happiness hinges on what they think of you. This is too weighty a burden for any child to bear.

The last point I'll make about selfless parenting is that if you don't take care of yourself overtly, then you're likely to meet your needs in unhealthy and covert ways, such as depression or anxiety. If you're depressed, people are going to take care of you. You end up getting medication, doctor visits, attention, time, and energy from other people. And so, in your attempt to be selfless, you have in fact engineered a way for yourself to be taken care of by other people. Your needs will be met one way or another. They will leak, they will scream, and they will awaken like Mr. Hyde if you do not learn how to attend to them.

SOURCES OF SUPPORT

You might wonder, "Should I attend therapy or Co-dependents Anonymous meetings for my son?" But the question is about *you*. If you need support, then you should go. There might be times when I'll tell a client, "Attend this meeting to help your child." But I'm also just as likely to say, "Then attend this other meeting for yourself." It's the oxygen masks on an airplane analogy again. Our natural instinct is to start helping another with his or her mask first and to hold our own breath while we do so. But if we fumble or if we pass out first, then neither of us gets the oxygen we need, and we're both doomed.

Years ago, I was working with a family whom I encouraged to attend a Co-Dependents Anonymous meeting together. The mother kept telling me, "I'm busy. I don't need to go to any meeting." Finally, I said, "I think you have to do this for yourself. You have to take care of yourself somehow. Your feelings leak out during our weekly phone calls. You're requiring a huge amount of support from me, and you required the same from your son when he was at home. It's not that I can't provide that support or don't want to provide that support, but it might not be the right kind of support. The fact of the matter is that you need a place where you can go and just talk about *you*. You need a place that's entirely about getting the support that you require."

"I can't go today," she replied. "I'm really not up for it. I need to pull myself together."

"No, you don't." I urged gently.

So without putting herself together, she walked into a meeting where people were there to provide support for a mother depleted from the burdens of raising a child suffering from addiction.

We all want to stay composed and strong. But sometimes the strongest thing is to admit you are vulnerable and need help. "Strong" is having the courage to walk into a room when you're a mess and to say, "I need help and support today." We're all human. We all require help sometimes. That doesn't make us weak.

We don't wait to go to the gym until we are in great shape. We go to the gym when we're struggling.

Go to individual therapy. Doing so does not mean that you have poor mental health. Where I come from, going to a therapist is often a sign of good mental health. But there are stigmas surrounding mental health, and we may have shame about asking for assistance. Some even feel shame when they have a physical ailment that needs to be attended to by a medical doctor. This is because many of us were taught from an early age that mental or physical weakness was a burden and thus was unappealing to others.

Books can be a huge source of support as well. Many of the self-help books I recommend for my clients are included in the reference section of this book. Remember, however, that it's important to strive to do this work for yourself. You're bettering yourself because it's the best thing you can do for *you*, and the changes you make will positively affect both you and your family.

Or it could be a metaphorical vacation, taking time away from focusing on your child's problems. As you struggle with your difficult

Take a vacation. This can be an actual vacation or just some time that you take for yourself during the day or over the weekend. child, ask yourself, "Do I need a vacation? Am I too attached? Am I living for myself or for someone else?" It's scary and hard. But you need to practice that in order to have enough gas in the tank to attend to your child. It's important to take time for yourself in order to be the healthiest person you can be and the best parent that you can be. So talk with a therapist or your partner or your friends about taking a literal or metaphorical vacation. Go to the movies. Exercise at the gym. Get a massage. Read for pleasure. Any kind of downtime can replenish the energy you desperately need to provide for others.

Another source of support is your higher power, or your fellowship if you belong to a church or a religious group. Try to find a way to believe that the universe will give you what you need. Because at the end of the day, you can do all that you can do, and I can do all that I can do to help you, but then we have to turn it over to something other than us. This faith or radical acceptance of what "is" can generate gratitude and leave us vigor for other areas where we need to grow.

PREPARING FOR RESISTANCE

It's not easy. Harriet Lerner described the energy of a system to return to status quo as "change back." This is the dynamic that one could expect after establishing a healthy new boundary in relationships. It is valuable to know that even our cherished loved ones will often resist change. Rare is the occasion when others celebrate our new boundaries, whether they are children, partners, friends, or work associates. Still, this awareness can prepare us for the ensuing pushback we get from our children when we set new boundaries. In fact, if everyone did what we requested without any resistance at all, we could miss an opportunity to grow.

At a graduation session with one family, I noticed how each member of the family took a blaming posture toward the other. Each was looking at another, pointing out a fault and asking that person to change. My final suggestion to them was, "Assume everyone else in the family is not going to change. Assume the others are going to continue to be their old idiot selves. From there you will have the focus on where it needs to be: squarely on yourself." Initially, the mother was angry with me, accusing me of being overly negative. I explained, "I am not being literal. I know all of you have made progress, but if you are expecting it to be easy, it is not going to work. You will end up fighting about who is doing what and how much. If you let go of the others' changing, you will all contribute a lot of positivity to the process."

We hope, of course, that our children will not push back against our positive changes forever. But when we first begin to change and improve, we often feel guilty. We feel responsible for the hurt, anger, and sense of betrayal our children may feel toward us because of the new boundary.

To move toward healthy parenting, we have to learn to feel the guilt and do the right thing for ourselves anyway or we will develop resentments and associated negative behaviors. If we can get our child to see the reasoning behind their actions and the effect of their choices on the family and themselves—good or bad—then they will not fight with us. But this is an abdication of our work and responsibility as a parent. It is a child's job to mess up, struggle, and seek the paths of least resistance; it is our job as parents to hold the line. In fact, part of child development depends on this dynamic in order for a child to foster a healthy sense of individuation and identity.

"One does not discover new lands without consenting to lose sight of the shore for a very long time." —André Gide

A close friend of mine, having thrived as a parent and created a context for her children in which they were able to find happiness and meaning in adulthood, told me once, "I had to deal with people who thought I was constantly doing the wrong thing with my children. Sometimes people offered their opinion and other times it was the messages from our culture. But I had to dig deep into myself to find what was true for me—what made sense. We weren't able to avoid pain and struggles, but our path led to a successful place for our children." Her words remind me that I have to pay attention to my children and myself and pay less attention to what our culture sometimes teaches us about parenting.

While as a therapist or parent educator I might be an expert in creating a process for you, *I don't know what you need to do, and you don't know what I need to do.* A mother recently confessed, "I have given up on my son going to Harvard. I just want him to go to college." She let out a laugh knowingly. "I am almost there. I am almost to the point where I can accept that I don't know what my son's path needs to be."

Following our children into the invitation to a new way of living requires us to either hold on tighter to those things that make us feel safe in the face of our fears and anxieties, or to let go of the known and embrace something entirely new. We embrace "what is" and understand the relationship we have with ourselves, as well as with others and their pain. When we deeply explore our past and what it has told us, we can finally take the leap to consider that it might not be the truth.

CONCLUSION

What we change inwardly will change our outer reality.

—Plutarch

SOME TIME AGO, I SAT BRAINSTORMING WITH ONE OF OUR managers at our program. He was struggling with chronic employee issues: morale, motivation, internal competition, and jealousy. Attempts to deal with these problems led to temporary relief, but eventually the issues resurfaced. His tone was pessimistic. Maybe, he thought, it was a personnel problem. Maybe we should set some tough boundaries, write up some of the offenses, and replace some people with more willing employees.

We discussed several possible solutions to the problems. As the discussion progressed, we identified some new approaches to deal with the challenges. The novelty of these fresh concepts led the manager to a renewed sense of optimism. This was my first warning that we were headed for more problems.

In the wilderness, you learn about powerlessness. Thunderstorms, windstorms, mosquitoes, cold fronts, heat, lost supply vehicles, or a student who throws a tantrum are all reminders that you are not in control. "You can only control what you can control" is a circular idiom that reminds us of the limits of our efforts. The field instructors teach students to "let go of the outcome," and the instructors must truly live this principle themselves if they have any expectation of working with adolescents for any significant length of time.

After the manager expressed his optimism about his new ideas, I gave him a reality check: "None of this is likely to work. It may all fail, and we will probably have to meet again in a couple of months to come up with some new ideas. And then those ideas probably won't work. But this is your job as a manager: you must constantly work toward productivity, employee retention, morale, and the program's success as a whole. As long as you keep doing that, then you will be a successful manager."

Similarly, one of the things that worries me when parents check in at our parent meetings with a sense of elation at the recent progress of their child is this false sense of control: "Things are going great. He has a job and has been sober for thirty days now. Fingers crossed!"

Of course we experience happiness when we see our children making progress, but I am often worried because I perceive that the parents' happiness is tied or contingent only on the child's progress rather than on their own growth. When a parent makes the turn toward focusing on what they can control, they embrace an enduring source of strength: "He is doing better with his work and depression, but the key is that I am going to therapy and have started spending more time with my friends. I am feeling stronger. I don't check in on him several times each day." Expanding on this idea, I want you to consider the following:

Everything in this book may not work.

And then you will read a different book, listen to a new philosophy, and discover a new principle in parenting. You will apply those concepts and they may also fail. You will continue this process indefinitely because this is your job as a parent. Viewing the process of parenting as an endless journey can help you maintain optimism, energy, and peace. It is a shift from the suffering that arises from the belief that it is possible to "arrive" at a desired outcome. What we often find when we surrender to the journey is that our external world begins to reflect the inner changes we make. And that can include our children benefitting and growing along with us.

WHAT IS THE MESSAGE OF HOPE?

Hope lies in two places: first, it lies within you. Hope, like happiness and all your other emotions, is your responsibility to maintain—not your child's. You will feel more optimistic when you focus on yourself and what *you* can control. You will be riddled with depression and anxiety if you focus on changing your child. Hold on to your child's successes and failures loosely; they cannot be the source of your hope and happiness.

Second, hope can come from realizing that as we journey toward a healthier, happier version of ourselves, we provide our children a context in our relationship that is more nurturing. We learn to love ourselves, learn to let go of fear, control, perfectionism, and shame. The manifestations of the fear and anxiety we feel are a harmful ingredient in our children's lives. We must learn to love our children with a love that does not suggest they need to be anything but themselves. Feeling they are broken or doomed sends harmful messages to them about who they are in this world. Consider the notion that you are not off course. The mistakes, pain, turmoil are all a part of the curriculum to help you discover new gifts and new insight. Embracing all of it will line you up with life.

A focus on what you can control does produce an outcome. A large majority of the families I work with experience success when they shift the focus to bettering themselves individually. Many of them experience setbacks, trials, and frustrations, but they share an overall sense that they are going in a healthier direction. Most of the students we treat in our wilderness program leave with an improved sense of self and a greater awareness of others. In the beginning they come to us begrudgingly, but by the end they shed tears of grief over leaving. Many of them express the sentiment that they want to come back to work for our program as a member of the staff, and about 25 percent of our current staff at any given time is comprised of former students. Many of my students send me their college entrance essays, in which they describe their experiences at our program, and I receive letters of gratitude and frequent positive updates from my former students.

I am constantly gratified to see change in our current students each day. Facilitating change in our lives and in our relationships, we subsequently require others to change. We learn to respond to only healthy interactions. We discard, ignore, or avoid reacting to others when they don't treat us with respect and kindness, and the result is that we only allow those in our lives who treat us well.

Salvador Minuchin writes that although one must be flexible to establish connection with clients, there is also a time to be the *immovable object*. The concept states that a person must take a position or a stance on a matter and require others to orient themselves in relation to that object. It is like the cornerstone of the house. All other angles in the house refer back to one angle.

If we change how we relate to ourselves and others, then we provide our children with a healthier environment. If we do this well, we give our children the ability to learn from us and respond to us and others in a healthy way. I have seen evidence of this in working with hundreds of clients, and even with my own friends and family.

I will return to where we started: with my life. Some time ago, I separated from my wife. I loved her then as I do now, but things were not working in our relationship. Therapy and other resources we were utilizing were not leading to the changes I wanted for my life. Separating was a terrifying decision to make, and one that my wife did not want. But I didn't like the man I was; I didn't like the father I was. I often found myself trying to do things in order to make my wife happy without considering our children's needs or my own.

I moved out of our family's home. I didn't do it perfectly, and I made a lot of mistakes, but I wanted a different life, a better life. I rented a condo nearby, and my son moved in with me. Not many people understood my decision, nor were they happy with it. My mother called me to tell me she thought I should go back home. "I don't believe in divorce," she told me, "and it is my job to tell you that you are making a big mistake." She repeated herself a few more times over the next few weeks, and I eventually had to tell her that I would not answer any more calls from her for a while. I told her I needed her love, support, and understanding, and if she could not provide me with that then I would not be willing to talk to her.

Around that same time, my therapist told me about the discussion she had with a Buddhist spiritualist who was a mentor of hers. This mentor shared with her the idea that sometimes we have to "kill our parents in order to grow up." He was talking about the metaphorical act of letting go of our parents and the expectations and ideas they have for us in order to free ourselves to be the best individuals that we can be. My therapist then added, "Sometimes we have to kill everybody in order to do that."

The truth is profound in this analogy. It is not a statement of violence or narcissism; it is a statement of liberation. What I found during this time was that many of the people who loved me made some changes in their own lives so that we could continue on with each other. My mother decided to go to therapy to work on herself and give me what I needed from her as a mother. She told me she was willing to be that loving and supportive person in my life, and I welcomed her on that journey.

A colleague and friend of mine, upon hearing of my separation, started in with a similar sentiment. She was a friend of both my wife and me, and she had a great deal of compassion for the pain my wife was experiencing. She was angry with me, and she let me know that through a series of text messages and e-mails. I care about and respect this friend, but I told her I would not be interested in continuing our friendship if she could not support the choices I had made. I told her that I only had space in my life for people who would love me the way I wanted and needed to be loved. I didn't need more experts in my life telling me about their version of my journey and how it should unfold, and so I released this friend from my life.

A number of weeks later, she came to me and asked if we could talk. She shared with me that she had gone back to her own therapist and done some very hard work regarding the divorce of her own parents and how my separation triggered feelings of resentment and pain within her. "I looked up to you," she admitted. "You were on a pedestal for me, and now you are back down on earth. That's been hard for me to accept." She then thanked me for challenging her, and said she had grown as a result of responding to my boundary. My wife and I have since reconciled and are enjoying our journey together. I am inspired by her remarkable strength and courage. She sets an example in vulnerability and willingness to change.

Many other friends and family members have since come forward to tell me that the changes I made in my life surrounding the separation had the same effect on them. Many shared that the shift I made in my relationships with them led them to do their own work. Even my wife says that our separation, though initially painful and scary, was a catalyst for positive change in her life. During this time, I learned who my true friends were. I learned what it meant to be a friend, and I tried to be a better one.

My wife has learned to take care of herself in a healthy way through this process. She is also a marriage and family therapist, and she's a very smart woman. Our relationship had turned into a mutual codependency, and it had us stuck. She now believes our separation was a blessing, and she has learned how to focus on change within herself in a way that therapy or books could never fully teach her. She now treats herself and me very differently. When I first left my home, my wife told me that she was sorry and that she would change, but this change took some time. And this is the only true instrument I know—change over time as measured in our interactions and behavior, not our words. Promises, apologies, or expressions of guilt don't mean anything until there is actual evidence in a person's behavior. I too walk with new steps and try to show up in our relationship as more present, authentic, and courageous. People ask me how life is now that we are back together and I cannot find words to describe the joy I feel to be in a relationship in which I can be me and it is okay.

Most importantly, our separation allowed me to be a better father to my children. Through the process I have learned to take care of my own needs, and as a result I can better attend to the needs of my children. On my good days, I am surer about myself and my children. I am learning to see them more clearly. I am learning how to offer them a more noncontingent love. I am learning to parent without shame or guilt and I am learning to offer compassion to myself and others. I am more aware of the many mistakes I continue to make and I have less shame about them than I used to.

One evening, right before I was to give a web lecture on parenting, I experienced a dilemma about my eighteen-year-old son. I had just returned from a business trip, and I found beer cans in the trash. I was angry and felt betrayed, and I wanted to punish him. I had trusted him to stay at my condo while I was away on business, and he had violated that trust. I called a friend and shared my anger with her. "I'm going to tell Jake that he has to move back in with his mother," I said. My friend then asked me a simple question: "What do you want for Jake?"

"Well," I replied. "First, I want him to have a successful life free of drug and alcohol problems. Second, I want to have a connection with him and an understanding that our relationship is built on trust."

"So tell him that," she said. And that was it. I went to his room and I asked him to go grocery shopping with me after my webinar. I didn't lecture him; I didn't ask for us to sit down and talk. (I have learned that one of the best ways to make our children shut down is to start with the lead-in, "We need to talk.") While walking down a grocery aisle, I simply told Jake that I found the beer cans and that I was angry. In a simple and short statement, I told him that I felt betrayed and that that feeling was mine to own. I told him that I was thinking about having him move back in with his mother since I would be traveling frequently over the next few weeks and that I didn't want to leave him alone, but that I also wanted to stay connected with him and keep a dialogue going. Then I ended the forty-five-second conversation and said, "I don't need to talk about it anymore. I just wanted to tell you what I was feeling and where I think this might have to go. Can you go and grab some milk and butter from the dairy aisle?"

When he came back, he started talking to me. He told me where the beer cans came from and described how he was struggling. We then started a dialogue about his struggle with alcohol and drugs, and a few months later he decided that complete abstinence was the only way he could be healthy and safe. Here is an excerpt from a letter he wrote to me the following Father's Day:

Just this year, my life has changed so much. I have only recently learned what a father-and-son relationship can be. Before, I was spinning out of control. I was stuck in a cycle where I would do something stupid, and then you would get angry or hurt and I would receive a consequence, and then I would fear you. After a while, the fear would fade, and then I'd do something stupid again, and the cycle would repeat. This happened many times, and I wish I understood sooner that it didn't have to be that way. I am sorry for the way I damaged our relationship in the past. It truly hurts when I think about how sorry I am. I now know what you wanted for me. I wish I knew then what I know now. If I did, I would have had a much more successful and happy adolescent period. The important thing is that I know it now. I can't imagine going off to college without the relationship that we have now. I think that there would be a large gap in my heart for the rest of my life. I can't thank you enough for everything you have given me. It has always been apparent to me that you made a goal to be a good dad. This you have done. I will never forget everything you have done for me, and I am more grateful than you know.

When I made the shift toward a healthier relationship with myself, my goal—perhaps for the first time in my life—was not to make anyone else change. I communicated clearly, set some new boundaries, and left it up to those around me to make their own choices. To be honest, I didn't think many of them would change. But I was happily proven wrong. My wife and I call our marriage "2.0" because we are in a new chapter, trying to live the principles of this book with each other. When we make positive changes within ourselves, there is hope for an optimistic outcome. This won't happen every time. Parents work tirelessly and courageously, and some of their children do not change for the better. But many children do. They care enough about you to see if the change is worth it, and often, they find out that it truly is.

At the beginning of this book we started with a concept from Campbell's *The Hero's Journey* in which the hero gets the call to adventure. In most cases this invitation is initially rejected. This is the part of the story when some parents stop and resist because, although the call comes in the form of a suffering child, it is terrifying to try new things. We are asked to leave so many things that make us feel safe and

THE JOURNEY OF THE HEROIC PARENT

comfortable. We are invited into sessions, treatment programs, and communication seminars to do family work. But because their children are in danger, many are eventually willing to answer the call and go into the darkness to face their fears. I once heard someone describe that thing we search for as we embark on the hero's journey as "the thing we cannot not do." As I have had the privilege of working with parents whose children are struggling, I know of no better way to describe the courage and motivation parents demonstrate as they embark on their heroic journey. They *must* do this. And they must forge their *own* passage. It is perilous, frightening, and painful. They worry about what people will say. Some people will deride and abandon them as they forge ahead, but these parents cross the threshold and bravely plunge into the unknown. They go in because their child is in there. They go in because they believe they are there to find their child and solve their problems. Then the question . . . what does the hero *really* discover at the end of the journey?

The epic story of Gilgamesh, perhaps one of the oldest surviving works of literature, speaks to every parent's journey. In the ancient Mesopotamian myth, Gilgamesh becomes distressed at the death of his friend Enkidu. Due to his suffering, Gilgamesh leaves his home and undertakes a long and perilous journey searching for the secret of eternal life. He endures many trials and tribulations on his quest. He swims to the bottom of the sea and retrieves the plan of immortality. When he resurfaces, he sets it down on the ground and while he bathes, the serpent steals it, and the sacred plan of immortality is lost. Yet as he travels home, he has his story to tell.

So what *does* the hero find? On his journey he finds the elixir of healing wisdom, something that he can share with others. We experience deep pain and develop compassion as we face the depths of our own struggles. And what we find is *our* story. We sit in groups, tell our stories, and listen to the stories of others. That is the message of this book. That is what I meant when I started with the concept that "the question is not the question." It is our struggling children and our willingness to ask different questions that reveal our authentic selves. The hero brings back her self: a deeper, richer version of herself. Loving your child is something you cannot *not* do. You will break and bleed. Old things will die in you and in their stead new ones will grow. And what you will have in the end is *your* story.

For me, even as a teacher, the elixir isn't always in the form of words. Some of what I have gleaned on my journey is difficult to put into words. That is because it is an experience rather than an explanation. You learn something by going though it that you cannot know any other way. My education and study has given me language, but being present on my painful and beautiful journey has carved out a place for more compassion toward others and myself.

I am honored to sit and offer some observations from the thousands of hero's journeys I have seen children and parents traverse. This is *my* story. This is *my* gift. This is also the gift that the remarkable, wonderful, struggling children and parents have given me. And I, in turn, give it back to you.

NOTES

FOREWORD

xvii **observation from Harvard anthropology professor:** Bahr, K. class syllabus, 1992.

xvii **Progress in wilderness therapy is dynamic:** For additional studies and research please see http://adolescents.snwp.com/additional-research.

xviii **Bronson and Merryman address:** Bronson, Po and Ashley Merryman, *NurtureShock: New Thinking About Children*. New York: Twelve, 2009.

CHAPTER ONE

6 **In their book, *Parenting from the Inside Out*:** Siegel, Daniel and Mary Hartzell, *Parenting from the Inside Out: How a Deeper Self-Understanding Can Help You Raise Children Who Thrive*. New York: Tarcher/Penguin, 2004, p. 1.

8 **This process begins with "knowing thyself.":** The ancient Greek aphorism "Know thyself" was inscribed in the forecourt of the Temple of Apollo at Delphi.

9 **Stephen A. Mitchell, in his book *Influence and Autonomy in Psychoanalysis*:** Mitchell, Stephen A. (1997). *Influence and Autonomy in Psychoanalysis*. Hillsdale, NJ: Analytic Press, 1997, p. xii, 61.

10 **Joseph Campbell, the renowned philosopher:** Campbell, Joseph, *Hero with a Thousand Faces*. London: Paladin, 1988.

CHAPTER TWO

15 **Viktor Frankl wrote in his harrowing memoir:** Frankl, Viktor E., *Man's Search for Meaning*. Boston: Beacon Press, 2006.

15 **As Thich Nhat Hanh explains:** Hanh, Thich Nhat, *You Are Here: Discovering the Magic of the Present Moment*. Boston: Shambhala Publications Inc., 2009.

16 **Carl Jung explains:** Jung, Carl, *Psychology and Religion*. New Haven, CT: Yale University Press, 1966; Jung, Carl and Aniela Jaffe, *Memories, Dreams, Reflections*. New York: Pantheon Books, 1963.

CHAPTER THREE

21 **lyrics by Kyle Henderson:** Henderson, Kyle, *"Puppet Will," Desert Noises*, (2012). Live recording at Audiotree Studio [electronic]. Chicago: Audiotree, 2012. (Available from http://audiotree.tv/session/desert-noises-session-2/)

22 **Dr. Jami Gill illustrates:** Gill, Jami D., *Finding Human*. North Charleston, SC: Create Space, 2014, p. 28.

25 **There are studies of infants:** Spitz, Rene A., *No and Yes: On the Genesis of Human Communication*. New York: International Universities Press, 1957.

25 **Harry Harlow's experiments showed:** Harlow, Harry F., "The Nature of Love." *American Psychologist* 13 (1958), 673–85.

27 **The book *Pain: The Gift Nobody Wants:*** Brand, Paul W. and Philip Yancey, *Pain: The Gift Nobody Wants*. New York: HarperCollins, 1993.

28 **Research indicates humans are:** Higgins, E. Tory, "Beyond Pleasure and Pain." *American Psychologist* 52(12) (1997), 1280–1300.

34 **Joseph Campbell gave his students:** Solomon, P. T. (producer & director), *Finding Joe* [motion picture]. USA: Balcony Releasing, 2011.

36 **Students of many disciplines learn Maslow's hierarchy of needs:** Maslow, Abraham H. (1943). "A Theory of Human Motivation," *Psychological Review* 50(4) (1943), 370–96.

38 **Dr. Daniel Siegel describes in his book:** Siegel, Daniel and Mary Hartzell, *Parenting from the Inside Out: How a Deeper Self-Understanding Can Help You Raise Children Who Thrive*. New York: Tarcher/Penguin, 2004.

CHAPTER FOUR

58 **Ultimately, Seth admitted:** I followed state requirements and reported the incident.

62 **He died in 1973:** Casals documentary [video file] (2008, January 12). Retrieved from www.youtube.com/watch?v=PdLCR_KYD7s&list=RDPdLCR_KYD7s.

CHAPTER FIVE

69 **Alice Miller warns us:** Miller, Alice, *The Drama of the Gifted Child: The Search for the True Self.* New York: Perennial, 1997.

69 **There's a story from the book *The One Minute Manager*:** Blanchard, Kenneth H. and Spencer Johnson, *The One Minute Manager.* New York: William Morrow and Company Inc., 1982.

74 **it is our attempt to solve:** Nichols, Michael P. and Richard C. Schwartz, *Family Therapy: Concepts and Methods* (2nd edition). Needham Heights, MA: Allyn and Bacon, 1991.

74 **Let's return to Jung's idea:** Jung, Carl, *Psychology and Religion.* New Haven, CT: Yale University Press, 1966; Jung, Carl and Aniela Jaffe, *Memories, Dreams, Reflections.* New York: Pantheon Books, 1963.

77 **In his biography of Steve Jobs:** Isaacson, Walter, *Steve Jobs.* New York: Simon & Schuster, 2011.

81–2 **"Even if we have come to understand ourselves well":** Siegel, Daniel and Mary Hartzell, *Parenting from the Inside Out: How a Deeper Self-Understanding Can Help You Raise Children Who Thrive.* New York: Tarcher/Penguin, 2004.

87 **in the literature of Joanna Bettmann:** Bettmann, Joanna, Keith C. Russell, and Kimber J. Parry, "How Substance Abuse Recovery Skills, Readiness to Change, and Symptom Reduction Impact Change Processes in Wilderness Therapy Participants." *Journal of Child and Family Studies,* 22(8) (2012), 1039–50.

91 **In his book *Nonviolent Communication: A Language of Life*:** Rosenberg, Marshall B., *Nonviolent Communication: A Language of Life* (2nd edition). Encinitas, CA: Puddle Dancer, 2003.

92 **the following quote by Henry T. Close:** Close, Henry. T. (1976). "On parenting" from *Voices: The Art and Science of Psychotherapy IV,* 1968.

93 **an article from the satirical publication *The Onion*:** "Study Finds Every Style of Parenting Produces Disturbed, Miserable Adults," *The Onion,* October 26, 2011, www.theonion.com/articles/study-finds-every-style-of-parenting-produces-dist,26452.

CHAPTER SIX

105 **Let's examine the Serenity Prayer:** Originally attributed to Reinhold Niebuhr and adapted by Alcoholics Anonymous, *Alcoholics Anonymous* (4th Edition). New York: A.A. World Services, 2011.

105 **A maxim from *The Parent's Handbook*:** Dinkmeyer, Don C., Sr. and Gary McKay, *Parenting Teenagers: Systematic Training for Effective Parenting of Teens.* Circle Pines, MN: AGS, 1998.

115 **Khalil Gibran's *The Prophet* reads:** Gibran, Khalil, *The Prophet.* London: Macmillan, 2010.

120 **There is an old saying:** Francis Skrenes. (n.d.). Library of Quotes.com. Retrieved from http://libraryofquotes.com/quote/925729.

121 **"Our children don't become":** Dayton, Tian., *Emotional Sobriety: From Relationship Trauma to Resilience and Balance.* Deerfield Beach, FL: Health Communications, 2007.

CHAPTER SEVEN

130 **From the story in Genesis:** Genesis 2:25, 3:7–11, King James Bible.

138 **Immanuel Kant wrote:** Kant, Immanuel, *Groundwork for the Metaphysics of Morals.* Berlin: Walter de Gruyter, 2006.

139 **In the book *The Anatomy of Peace*:** Arbinger Institute, *Anatomy of Peace: How to Resolve the Heart of Conflict.* London: Penguin, 2010, 125-26.

142 **Buddha said, "Hatred does not cease by hatred":** As cited in Gill, Jami D., *Finding Human.* North Charleston, SC: Create Space, 2014.

147 **Harriet Lerner illustrates this in *The Dance of Anger*:** Lerner, Harriet G., *The Dance of Anger: A Woman's Guide to Changing the Patterns of Intimate Relationships.* New York: Perennial Currents, 2005.

147 **These are the dragons Campbell identifies:** Campbell, Joseph, *Hero with a Thousand Faces.* London: Paladin, 1988.

148 **My therapist has a poster:** Image courtesy of Jami D. Gill. Printed with permission.

148 **As depicted in the eponymous movie:** Mahatma Ghandi, *Gandhi*, directed by Richard Attenboroug. Columbia Pictures, 1982.

149 **A more simple illustration:** Image courtesy of Doug Savage. Printed with permission.

154 **C. S. Lewis explained this way:** Lewis, C. S., *Mere Christianity*. New York: HarperCollins, 2001.

155 **D. W. Winnicott attempted to remove:** Grolnick, Simon A., *Work and Play of Winnicott*. Northvale, NJ: Jason Aronson, 2010.

CHAPTER EIGHT

162 **In *The Drama of the Gifted Child*, Alice Miller writes:** Miller, Alice, *The Drama of the Gifted Child: The Search for the True Self.* New York: Perennial, 1997.

163 **a story from Pulitzer Prize–nominated writer David Foster Wallace:** http://www.youtube.com/watch?feature=player_embedded&v=PhhC_N6Bm_s.

163 **In the book *The Narcissism Epidemic*:** Twenge, Jean M. and W. Keith Campbell, *The Narcissism Epidemic: Living in the Age of Entitlement*. New York: Free Press, 2009.

165 **Jessica Benjamin wrote:** Benjamin, Jessica, *The Bonds of Love: Psychoanalysis, Feminism, and the Problem of Domination*. New York: Pantheon Books, 1988.

168 **During a lecture for parents of young adults:** Pearlmutter, K., personal communication, April 26, 2013.

169 **Richard Bach, in his book *Illusions*:** Bach, Richard, *Illusions: The Adventure of a Reluctant Messiah*. London: Arrow Books, 1976, p. 109.

177 **My mentor, Dr. Leslie Feinauer, said:** Feinauer, Leslie, personal communication, 1995.

178 **Viktor Frankl illuminated:** Frankl, Viktor E., *Man's Search for Meaning*. Boston: Beacon Press, 2006.

180 **In the song "Defying Gravity,":** Schwartz, S. (music & lyrics) & Holzman, W. (writer). (2003). *Wicked: The Untold Story of the Witches of Oz* [Broadway play]. New York: Universal Pictures.

CHAPTER NINE

182 **Jessica Benjamin put it this way:** Benjamin, Jessica, *The Bonds of Love: Psychoanalysis, Feminism, and the Problem of Domination*. New York: Pantheon Books, 1988.

189 **Murray Bowen calls this dynamic *triangulation*:** Bowen, Murray, *Family Therapy in Clinical Practice*. New York: Aronson, 1978.

190 **Bowen suggests working through:** Ibid.
195 **Salvador Minuchin, a pioneer in family therapy:** Minuchin, Salvador
and H. Charles Fishman, *Family Therapy Techniques*. Cambridge, MA.:
Harvard University Press, 1981.

CHAPTER TEN

200 **Here is a discussion of some parent rights:** McMahon, Tom, *Teen Tips:
A Practical Survival Guide for Parents with Kids 11–19*. New York: Pocket
Books, 1996.
202 **A friend of mine who teaches:** Nelson, J., personal communication, 2014.
206 **Harriet Lerner described the energy:** Lerner, Harriet G., *The Dance of
Anger: A Woman's Guide to Changing the Patterns of Intimate Relationships*.
New York: Perennial Currents, 2005.
207 **"One does not discover":** Andre Gide quote found on http://www
.brainyquote.com/quotes/keywords/shore.html.

CONCLUSION

212 **Salvador Minuchin writes:** Minuchin, Salvador and H. Charles Fishman, *Family Therapy Techniques*. Cambridge, MA.: Harvard University
Press, 1981.
216 **Here is an excerpt from a letter:** Reedy, personal communication, 2011.
218 **I once heard someone describe:** Solomon, P. T. (producer & director),
Finding Joe [motion picture]. USA: Balcony Releasing, 2011.
218 **The epic story of Gilgamesh:** Ziolkowski, Theodore, *Gilgamesh Among
Us: Modern Encounters with the Ancient Epic*. Ithaca, NY: Cornell University Press, 2011.

QUESTIONS FOR HEROIC PARENTING

As we struggle to parent a child with mental health and addiction issues, it is crucial that we ask ourselves courageous questions. These questions lead to the transformation where we understand the effects of our behaviors on others and on ourselves. Pure accountability asks for nothing in return. The following list of questions may be helpful as you consider your behavior as it relates to your child and can lead to greater connection to ourselves and loved ones.

- What am I feeling?
- Do I own my feelings or am I blaming my child or others for my feelings?
- Why am I sharing my feelings with my child? Am I asking them to change so my feelings will change?
- Can I let my child hate me or be angry with me? Am I asking my child to provide me with unconditional love?
- Can I let my child struggle with an issue without me needing to solve it?
- Am I obsessing about other's faults (my child, my co-parent)?
- What is my part in the problem?
- What am I doing to take care of myself?

- Why don't I know the answer to my question, "What should I do?" What is in the way of me accessing my truth and my authenticity?
- Do I feel punished or judged when a mentor, therapist or coach provides me with feedback?
- Can I look at my mistakes without feelings of shame and guilt?
- Can I laugh at myself? Can I let others laugh at me?
- Are my questions really statements or is my statement really a question?
- Am I asking questions of my child to get information or to shame or guilt them into saying the right thing?
- Am I lecturing, guilting, yelling, pleading, whining, nagging, complaining so I don't have to set a boundary?
- Do I use fear or do I try to scare my child into doing the right thing?
- Do I lie or stretch the truth to try to control how my child feels or what he or she thinks?
- Do I think I know my child's truth or am I helping them to find it for themselves?
- Do I read about parenting skills, tools and principles so I can figure out how to change my child or do I want to learn, expand and grow as a parent?
- Does saying sorry cause me to feel defeated or less than?
- Do I think I have to be a perfect parent?
- Have I made sense and explored my own childhood enough to know there are some areas where I am blind or limited?
- If my child's behavior could speak, what would it say to me?
- What are the benefits of my or my child's maladaptive behaviors?
- If I were my child, what would be my complaints about my parenting? Consider creating this list and sharing it with your child and asking for feedback.

PARENTING MANTRAS

As children, our minds were hardwired by our experiences and our context. Our parents and our culture taught us how to be in this world, how to belong. Because this training is so powerful and pervasive, and because many messages were taught without words or before we had the capacity to catalog them in the verbal parts of our brain, one-time insights and epiphanies don't often have lasting effects. Change requires us to practice, repeat and walk into the face of those old messages. One resource that might help us to combat old scripts can be a mantra we repeat to ourselves. In the face of fear, guilt, or shame, we often have to practice new behavior long before those debilitating feelings and old messages lose their power over us. From the following list of mantras, you may find messages you can repeat to yourself to help you battle the old ghosts and voices from your past.

- What I feel matters.
- I don't have to be right.
- "No" is sometimes a complete sentence.
- I can tell others I don't want to talk about it.
- I can take care of myself and that doesn't mean I am selfish.

- What someone thinks about me is his or her business.
- Anxiety and fear lie to me. They tell me I am not okay and that I have to control things to be okay.
- Authenticity is more important than how others see me.
- With regard to events and set backs in life, good is good and bad is good.
- I will listen, understand, and connect to my child. I do not have to respond, change, or fix his or her feelings.
- I will use I statements rather than arguing objective truths and using imperatives (right, wrong, good, bad, have to, need to, should, ought to).
- I have a right to ask professionals tough questions and to question what they advise me.
- I will evaluate my parenting through thoughtful self-examination and with the help of trusted peers and professionals.
- Difficult emotions are a part of life and I will avoid trying to fix them in others and in myself.
- I will remind myself that the detours are part of the journey.
- Unnecessary suffering comes because I have not embraced the journey I am on with my child and others.
- I will make my serenity my responsibility, not my child's.
- I will own my emotions and allow others to own theirs by mindfully listening to them.
- Symptoms in others and myself are evidence of our wounds.
- I will run the expressed or unexpressed thoughts and feelings of my child through my adult filter and make decisions informed by more than just my child's wishes.
- I will not evaluate my parenting in reference to what my culture tells me is the right way to do it.
- I will not let guilt and shame guide me in finding my truth.
- I will question the messages from my early childhood context.
- I will not abdicate my responsibility in making decisions to professionals, but I will use professionals to gain information and help me to be clear.

- I will not evaluate my parenting by reference to my child's successes or failures.
- I will let my child solve their problems and will commit to recognizing what is my problem and what is their problem.
- I will look for the gifts that come with the challenges of raising a child who struggles with mental health or addiction issues.
- I will do my work, even if my child is functioning well. I will continue to learn throughout my life, even if my child is not struggling.
- Need and love are not the same thing.
- Compliments are not love.
- Connection, understanding and seeing my child's whole self are more important to the improvement of his or her self-esteem than praise.
- The more I can see all the parts of myself, the more I will be able to see others.
- Success and failures are critical elements in learning for my child and me.
- I don't need my child to be a certain way for me to love them.
- I am responsible for the trust I extend and the forgiveness I offer—the same is true for my child.
- Forgiveness comes on the terms of the offended, not on the terms and timeline of the offender.
- Trust is mine to give or not—there is no objective level of behavior that can dictate when trust is to be given.
- My parents weren't perfect. They were compromised and limited in some respects and I can both see that and love them.
- I am still a child, in many ways, and my imperfect self is perfect.

dan at city ventures.com

- what therapy methods?
- Lyndsey
- Kelley/Dad's intervention offer
- Esme said she's fine either way (divorce/no divorce)
- Something to write on a note for Esme on her trip
- Sleep issues - dealing w/ internal pain/shame

---

ask yourself each day about yes or no to divorce.

- Its devestating to me that you make these choices.
* Changes - outpatient program